Equestrian Chess

Clay Pigeon Racing

Cross Country Standing

Rugby League

Pub Talk

Roller-knitting

Salop Nun-Rolling

Course Snouting

Coming soon

D1580092

Winchester Frottage, Chimp, Scandinavian Plankpuck, Trumpy, Crown Green Fumbling, Cock-a-Hoop, Motorised Basque Fiasco, Association Gimp, Gloucestershire Troll-Baiting, Fell Chaffing, Old Time Tussock and Guff, Sequence Gazebo, Devil-take-the-Thimble, Dutchman's Douche, Kwok, Equestrian Chess, Sports Injuries: Joints and Clefts, Old-Time Camping, Filch, Bidet & Peep, Cross Country Standing, Keeping Fit In The Kitchen, Greco-Roman Antics, Pub Talk, Eton Squeeze, Carpet Malarkey, Svenbender, Downhill Shooting, Rolf, Fuddlehump, Table Thrush, Portaloo, Scrabbage, High Camping, Flat Pank, Deepwater Lurking, Dorset Flaps, Alpine Fol-de-rol, Arson For Insurance Purposes, Stool Billiards, Shove-bugger, Disorienteering, Himmel Smeer Blindman's Grubb, Four-Door Doris, Tickle-the-Goose (Latin-style), Girdletwang Clinging, Lawn Tufty, Scab & Pluck, Shanghai Prong, Quiff, Contract Sludge, New South Wales Ringpull, Waterboarding

More titles added the minute we can think of them.

Conkers for Goalposts

First published in the United Kingdom in 2010 by
Portico Books
10 Southcombe Street
London
W14 0RA

An imprint of Anova Books Company Ltd
Copyright © Harry Pearson 2010
Illustration by Tim Bradford
Designed by Doug Cheeseman
The moral right of the author has been asserted.

ISBN 9781906032630
A CIP catalogue record for this book is available from the British Library.
10 9 8 7 6 5 4 3 2 1

Printed and bound by 1010 Printing International Ltd, China

This book can be ordered direct from your publisher at anovabooks.com

Conkers for Goalposts

Gathered together for the first time under one cover – five of Tackle This Sport's most popular titles:

PORTICO

tackle
this sport

Foreword

by sporting legend Barry Wardrobe, star of TV's It's A Knockout & The World's Strongest Man

To be fair, reading has never really been my bag. The only book I've regularly had in my hands in the past three decades is the telephone directory – and that's only preparatory to tearing it in half on *The World's Strongest Man*.

The one exception to that is the Tackle This Sport series, a collection of guides that were to become a multi-coloured bible to a certain junior yours truly back in the days when Barry Wardrobe was still just an unknown spotty-faced but hard-grafting and 150 per cent focused Herbert taking his first tentative steps on the uphill path strewn with broken dreams that leads to the first rung of the rickety ladder marked "Sporting Legends – This Way".

As I say, I can't remember exactly when I first came across a Tackle This Sport volume, where I was at the time, or which of the 537 fascinating and informatively practical titles it was I first grasped in my chalk-coated mitts. But you can rest assured that, like the true professional I am, I didn't let that make me take my eyes off the prize for a second when my agent came on the blower and said there was 200 quid available to anyone who was prepared to gabble on the topic for ten minutes to some Percy from the publishers.

So let's put it this way – ever since that day, whenever and wherever it was, the TSP series has always been my blue touchstone. Something I know will light me up whenever the wheels have come off and I need to step up a gear and turn on the big fireworks. Where would I have been without such classics as *Beginners Leotard*, or *Graeco-Roman Boasting*? Not smiling bitterly after finishing runner-up in the BBC Sports Personality of the Year behind Northamptonshire's David Steele, that's for certain.

No, whether he's been storming out of European Superstars after a judging fiasco vis-à-vis the legitimacy of my burpas, leading Shrewsbury to victory in the vital penguin-on-a-sliding-conveyor-belt game in the Ghent qualifier of *Jeux Sans Frontiers*, or standing in for Mr Ron Pickering (a big man in every sense of the word) as presenter of *We Are The Champions*, or simply promoting my unique Boar-Grappler™ work-out tool with a nationwide tour of sports centres, Barry Wardrobe has always been aware that if it hadn't been for that fateful morning, afternoon or evening when I got that first copy of TSP out of the library, or for a Christmas present from my Nan, it might all have been very, very different.

So it's absolutely terrific in the humble opinion of this so-called sporting great that after donkey's years the five most popular titles in the Tackle This Sport Series series are now being made available again in the sort of chunky volume even B Wardrobe esquire would struggle to fling over the roof of a bowling alley for a sponsored charity event in aid of kiddies. Let's just hope we will soon see this terrific book along with companion volumes taking pride of place on the shelves of charity shops across Britain just like in the great old days of yore.

The people who know me best tell me they don't believe the world is big enough to take another Barry Wardrobe. That's probably true. But if even half a Barry Wardrobe emerges as a result of this book, then the sporting life in this great country we call Team GB will be all the better for it. Now, stop fannying around, pull your finger out, get up off your backsides and Tackle This Sport!

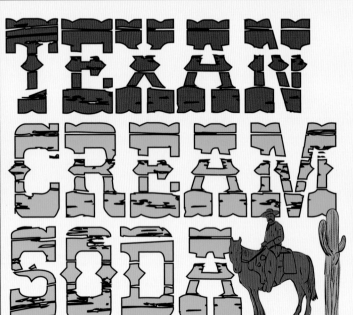

The Basics

Playground fighting is a martial art in which the fighters battle to assert their supremacy over one another using holds, throws and bags of midget gems. Manoeuvring, speed and stamina all play their part, as does a range of fighting weapons such as "the satchel and the geography book".

Dating back to Ancient Greece where men liked nothing better than to throw another man to the ground and then sit on his chest, the sport developed through the centuries with the Vikings, the Huns and the Mongol horde of Gengis Khan all helping to popularise it.

By the Middle Ages playground fighting was the national pastime of Merry England and Henry VIII even banned football for fear that it would lure young men away from playground fighting and turn his kingdom into a land of long-haired, hugging and kissing, preening, vain jessies.

During the Puritan era Oliver Cromwell, who felt that playground fighting wasted energy that could be put to better use torturing the Irish, outlawed it. However the sport was kept alive by a body of brave enthusiasts who carried on playground fighting in secret. To this day many old stately homes in England still have a secret playground fighting arena, often hidden in the attic, or behind an old clock. In this age of do-gooders and namby-pamby social workers who is to say that they won't soon be needed again!

It was in Victorian times that playground fighting as we know it today really developed at English public schools such as Beasts College and Saint Brute's, Windor. Spurred on by the need to

The fight

produce the leaders of Empire many top schools made playground fighting compulsory, building into it a code of honour that would instil in the playground fighters a sense of decency and fair-play that at the same time did not preclude them from marching into someone else's country and forcing the native inhabitants to bring them plentiful food and drink. As the poet A.E. Pederast, a former housemaster of Saint Brute's, noted: "Playground fighting is so much more than just a game. It is an all-encompassing experience that forges men from boys and leaves an indelible legacy of pluck, coolness and secret bedwetting".

To this day playground fighters always show deep respect to one another even when abusing each other's mothers. For this reason it is often said that playground fighting is as much a philosophy as a way of getting somebody to give you their last fudge finger by twisting their wrist until they cry.

As the American writer Mr Norman Mailer, a great aficionado of playground fighting, wrote after watching the legendary Harlem playground fighter Du'la'Kev Bristow perform a perfect wedgie on his opponent: "In playground fighting a man has his honour and he has his pants and sometimes his honour is his pants and sometimes his pants are his honour, but just occasionally, in those great transcendent moments when strength and skill combine to lift the physical out from the realms of the merely metaphysical a man's pants are simply his pants – and that is the gaping existential rift that faces all men, even those of us with enormous talent and implausibly huge genitals." This, then, is very much the world of playground fighting.

Equipment

SNAKE BELT – All playground fighters wear a snakebelt. The different colours denote the skill and experience of the combatant. These range from claret-and-blue for the champion fighter to plain yellow for that chubby boy in the cardigan who prefers to do skipping with the girls.

Champion

Trainee

TIE – Traditionally made from the finest polyester, the tie is worn loosely round the fighter's neck.

Chubby boy in cardigan

The size of the knot of the tie is a second indicator of the fighter's experience level with the bigger the knot the better. The highest grade of playground fighter is a claret-and-blue belt Jason King knot. During bouts fighters will often attempt to shrink their opponents knots by pulling on the tie ends. If they succeed it gives them an important psychological advantage.

ANORAK – Worn only during the warm-up and when entering the ring. The anorak is traditionally worn as a cape with the hood up. The sleeves are purely ceremonial. Some younger fighters prefer a snorkel parka though this is still outlawed by some playground fighting associations for "making you look like a bloody Eskimo".

SANDALS – Footwear that declares the owner is a playground-fighting pacifist. It is against all the rules of playground fighting to engage anyone who wears sandals in an actual bout, though you may on occasion be allowed to run up, kick them and then run away again.

BLAKEYS – Metal segments (sometimes called segs) that are nailed into the sole of the fighter's shoe by his granddad "to stop you wearing the

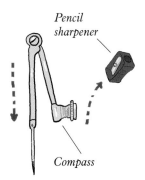

Pencil sharpener

Compass

blessed heels down in two minutes flat". They offer a better grip, the psychological boost of being able to produce sparks when sliding and can be highly effective when deployed in a finger stamp.

HAVERSACK – Traditionally either Army surplus khaki or RAF blue with the fighter's name painted on the flap using some leftover gloss emulsion Dad had in the shed. May also be adorned with other runic slogans for example "Leeds Rule", "T Rex R Puffs" and "Slade". When swung by its longest strap the haversack is a useful medium-range weapon especially when filled with six volumes of the SMP Maths books and Longmans audio-visual French livre trois.

COMPASS – A lethal close-quarters weapon that is never used in an actual fight, but is often deployed in the preliminary "maths lesson" phase of a bout. This occurs when one fighter issues a silent challenge to his opponent by jabbing the compass into his buttocks when he is in the middle of trying to do a complicated bit of long division. The opponent accepts the challenge by picking up a pencil sharpener and throwing it at the challenger's head, or rejects the challenge by screaming and yelling "Sir, sir, sir! He's sticking me in the arse, sir."

RULER – An alternative "challenge issuer" to the compass. Generally employed two-handed with one hand holding the ruler firmly while the other bends it back and then lets go, so that the ruler flicks forward and strikes the challenged opponent on the back of the head. Some expert fighters use the ruler to issue a long-range challenge, using the "Catty" flick, which employs the method described above with the addition of a chunk of blotting paper liberally soaked with watery ink or spittle.

The Fighter

Tie

Turkish puzzle ring

Snake belt

Haversack

Shirt (un-tucked)

Trousers (tucked)

DRESS

His belt and tie show that this combatant is a sky-and-dark-blue belt, mummy-tied-it knot – in other words a medium-grade fighter. He carries the lighter type of haversack that contains only exercise books, a tin of technical drawing pens and a slide rule. Such a bag is used to deliver a flurry of swift blows designed to confuse an opponent rather than stun him (for that he would need to add a Bible, or a full packed lunch including a Thermos of soup).

The shirt is worn un-tucked for greater freedom of movement. The trousers are tucked inside the Chelsea boots in homage to the crew of the Starship Enterprise, suggesting that this fighter might be hoping to employ a "Mr Spock" (*see The Moves*). Note the Turkish puzzle ring on the third finger of the fighter's right hand. This will have to be removed before the contest begins or he will be instantly disqualified for acting "like a dirty foreigner".

The Arenas

Fight in progress

Teacher on yard duty

Lookout

Girls skipping

Dinner lady
(with upset littlies)

OUTDOOR – Playground. Note markings for at least seventeen different sports: netball, basketball, five-a-side, hockey, hopscotch, shot-putt circle, polo, gridiron, cricket, British bulldog etc.

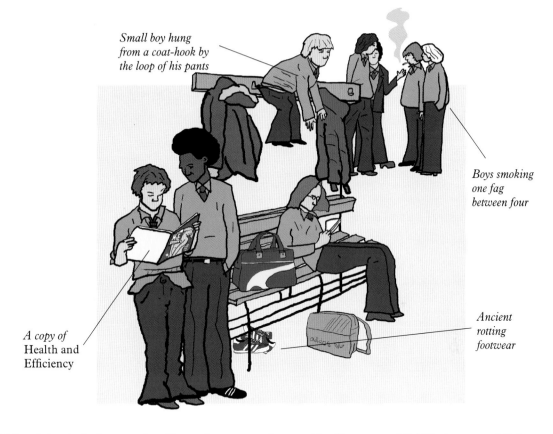

Small boy hung from a coat-hook by the loop of his pants

Boys smoking one fag between four

A copy of Health and Efficiency

Ancient rotting footwear

INDOOR – School cloakroom. An all-weather venue, favoured by Xtreme and RAW playground fighters.

Etiquette & Ritual

Playground fighting is unique in that it is the only martial sport that shuns the idea of weight categories. In PGF even the tiniest participant can find him or herself stepping into the famous screeching human circle against a 42-stone giant (or Big Fatty as the larger fighter is traditionally known). In fact nine times out of ten that's exactly what happens.

As in many other martial arts, combat in PGF is preceded by a series of rituals. In sumo there is the throwing of salt, likewise in playground fighting we have the hurling of insults. These come in many forms but for the beginner the easiest and most effective is probably "In the bush" (A truncated version of the original Elizabethan insult famously yelled by Merkin in Ben Jonson's comedy *Oops There Go-eth My Pantaloons!* "As to your mother, Sir; a country bawd of most lowly aspect, unable to afford bed, chair or palliasse, she serves her clients amongst the shrubs and the grasses").

When the opening ceremony is finished the non-combatants form the famous human ring and

The Circle

Glasses
Jumper
Mug
Cords
Patches
Hush Puppies

The Weigh-in   *The Timekeeper*   *The Reconciliation*

begin the age-old chant of "Fight! Fight! Fight!" or for the gang rumble "All join on/No girls on".

The circle plays an important role (*see rules over page*) one of which is keeping watch for the approach of the timekeeper (easily distinguished by his ceremonial coffee mug, leather elbow patches and the particles of sacred digestive biscuits which decorate the front of his jumper). The ring signals his approach with a hissing noise and stage whispers of "Nix, nix. It's Puffy Padmore".

The arrival of the timekeeper and his cry of "What on earth's going on? You could hear your infernal racket in the staff-room even after we shut the windows," signals the end of the bout.

After a fight, no matter what the outcome, the two participants join together in a time-honoured ceremony of reconciliation – sharing a bag of sweet 'n' sour Nik-Naks and then both taking swigs out of a bottle of lurid green fizzy pop.

Thus, as the great Japanese playground fighter Shoji Ono wrote in 1625, "are the fighting spirits of the two warriors joined together in brotherhood by the mutual exchange of one another's crumbs".

The Rules

To the untutored eye playground fighting may look like a real free-for-all, but the contest is actually fought out to a series of rigid and strictly enforced rules. Unique amongst sports PGF does not have umpires or referees; rather the fighters themselves and the spectators who form the human ring enforce the rules.

The spectators in particular keep a careful eye out for infringements, which they then point out with a cry of "Away, man [name of fighter] you dirty get". If other members of the human ring agree with this call they will assent with shout of "Yeah, cut it out [name of fighter] or we're all piling in". If however another spectator disagrees with the call he or she may intervene by yelling "Shut your mouth, you". The dispute is then resolved by a reasoned discourse over which of the two has the bigger brother.

OFFENCES

The human ring is particularly looking out for:

KICK-A-DONKEY – The kicking of an opponent with the toe is the worst offence a fighter can commit, as it is cowardly and foreign. Kicking is strictly forbidden except in the case of the Kwai Chang Caine. (*see The Moves*)

HAIR-PULLING – One of the so-called "girly moves" that are outlawed in all playground fights, except if the fighters are girls in which case they can do what they want, really.

SHOUTING – There is nothing in general wrong with a bit of shouting. Indeed using Tarzan's war cry, or imitating the call of a peacock are often an integral part of the playground fight. However, the judges may intervene if they feel one of the fighters is deliberately making a lot of noise in order to attract the attentions of a dinner lady.

EAR GRAB – Highly popular with teachers and irate mothers, the ear grab, which involves seizing a fighter by the ear, twisting it slightly and then dragging him away by it to the headmaster's study/get his tea because I'll be beggared if I'm going to labour over a hot stove all day so you can ignore me when I shout for you, you little twerp, is frowned upon in playground fighting.

SLAPS AND SCRATCHES – Another "girly move". Persistent slaps and hair-pulling sometimes land the fighter with a punitive "sissy" ban. Nobody will fight a sissy. Not even his sister.

JUDGING

As well as looking out for infringements the human ring is also there to judge who has won the fight and put a stop to it.

A fighter is defeated if:

(a) He cries (although later he will claim that he wasn't – he had just got some dirt in his eye).

(b) He threatens to get his Dad.

(c) He feigns serious injury, limping around and shouting, "If my leg wasn't bust I'd bash you up".

(d) He is pinned to the ground by his opponent sitting on his chest for the full length of an episode of *Wacky Races*.

(e) He surrenders with the full submission call: "Ayah-Ayah-Ayah".

When a fighter does any of these things the human ring moves to end the contest saying, "Leave him alone now. He's had enough" and then wandering off to throw cinders at pigeons.

Silent Insults and Challenges

The Hurling of Insults

Quite often the situation does not allow for verbal insults or challenges, for example it is impossible to call into question the sexual preferences of somebody's shoes during double physics if "Puffy" Padmore is making you do a test on the laws of velocity. When quiet is called for the experienced playground fighter can get his message across using a series of internationally recognised gestures.

THE JIMMY HILL

The challenger inserts his tongue in the flap between his bottom lip and his lower jaw and slowly strokes the tip of his chin while nodding in the direction of his rival.

THE NOSE SCRATCH AGINCOURT

The traditional British V-sign originated during the 100 Years War. Here this ancient martial gesture is stealthily directed towards a rival while apparently tackling an itch on the nostril.

THE DOUBLE NOSE SCRATCH AGINCOURT

As above but on this occasion the playground fighter doubles the power of his insult by tackling both itchy nostrils simultaneously.

THE DATE

In this challenge the playground fighter lays out the full details of the coming contest by a sequence of hand signals.

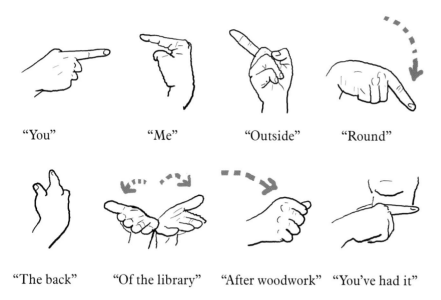

"You" "Me" "Outside" "Round"

"The back" "Of the library" "After woodwork" "You've had it"

His rival then responds by pointing at his knees and waggling them from side to side while sarcastically imitating a terrified old lady.

The Moves

Going directly for the coccyx – a sound tactic

Nipping is illegal. Remember: You must grip muscle as well as skin

In combat playground fighters use a wide variety of fast, cunning and sadistic moves:

THE NAG

The opponent's arm is twisted behind his back. Once he is securely held the attacker begins to sing the nursery rhyme "Horsey, horsey, don't you stop", kneeing his adversary rhythmically in the buttocks during the "clippety-clop" bit.

THE NINJA

Also known as "the horse bite" in parts of East Anglia, the Ninja is a move that relies on speed and surprise. Feinting to grab the opponent's ear, nose or lunchbox, the attacker drops his hand and instead grabs the soft tissue above his adversary's knee, squeezing it hard between thumb and fore-finger while intoning, "Ninja, ninja, ninja" in a vague approximation of a sinister Japanese accent.

Try this in an official bout and you will be disqualified!

The target is the thigh! Only a coward, or Inspector Jack Regan, aims for a more frontal area.

THE DNL

The deadly nipple lock, a vicious pinch with twisting motion administered to the chestal region, is now officially banned by the FIBCR, however it is still legal in Xtreme Playground Fighting, a variation of the sport rapidly gaining in popularity in the USA and parts of South London.

THE HIGHLAND BUTT

First recorded in the Jacobite Rebellion of 1745 and subsequently popularised by Leeds United, this is a forceful and dynamic assault in which the attacker hops forward rapidly on one leg with the other leg bent and applies his knee with full force to his opponent's upper thigh while yelling, "Sassenach!"

The KCC – foreign yet effective

The rabid dog look can give a fighter an important "mental" edge

THE KWAI CHANG CAINE

Kicking is usually illegal in playground fighting but following the success of the *Kung Fu* TV series starring David Carradine a new move involving a kick has been legitimised by FIBCR. To register as a legal KCC the kick must:

(a) Be delivered with the sole of the foot not the toe or instep.

(b) Must be preceded by the deliverer making a series of complex hand gestures before shouting "So, Glasshopper!" in a silly accent.

(c) Must be accompanied by an oriental sounding noise e.g "Ha-WAAH!"

THE MAD DOG

More a psychological ploy than a fighting move, the mad dog may unnerve and disarm even the toughest opponent, if they have never encountered it before. To achieve the mad dog, the fighter sneaks into the dining room shortly before his bout and fills his cheeks with semolina pudding. Then as the fight commences he should let out a series of growling noises and begin rolling his eyes while gradually allowing the semolina to ooze out of the sides of his mouth. The move is finished off by the opponent howling as "foam" drips down his chin, and then leaping forward as if to bite.

It's all in the wrist action!

THE MR SPOCK

Named in honour of the semi-alien officer from *Star Trek* the Mr Spock is a modified Vulcan Death Grip. The attacker forms both his hands into crab-like pincers much like those employed in the ninja, then swiftly manoeuvres himself onto the blindside of his opponent (possibly by shouting, "Blimey, look over there. It's a nudist woman on a motorbike"). He then grips the tops of his foe's shoulders while murmuring, "Totally illogical, Captain".

THE BATTLING TOP

Deployed by a fighter armed with a satchel or haversack. The fighter extends the arm holding his bag and simply whirls round and round letting centrifugal force do the rest. Should his opponent survive the Battling Top the fighter who has employed it uses his reeling dizziness for defensive purposes.

THE FULL AYA-AYA-AYA WITH KECKS DROP DRUMMING

This is arguably the most spectacular move of all and certainly the one that most excites playground fighting aficionados. In a complex series of manoeuvres the fighter first gets his opponent's head under his arm (known as the half aya-aya-aya *fig. 1*). Having rubbed his knuckles brutally over his adversary's crown (a full aya-aya-aya *fig. 2*), he then executes a switch of position that allows him to pull his opponent's trousers down exposing his pants and the top half of his bum to a panel of judges made up of teenage girls who have spent the afternoon in the reverent contemplation of photos of male pop stars, the sniffing of nail varnish and imbibing the sacred Co-op own-brand sweet vermouth (*fig. 3*).

Points are awarded according to the decibel level of the cackling that follows the kecks-drop, though a fight can be instantly stopped if any judge feels that the move was perfectly executed. Should this be the case she signals the fact by rushing across the hall, removing a white sling-back and beating out a rhythm on the exposed flesh of the defeated fighter while screeching "Umbongo, Umbongo, they drink it in the Congo. Eee, I'm mental, me!"

Figure 1

Figure 2

The sudden switch of headlock position and swift pulling down of pants is one of the most breathtaking manoeuvres in this superb sport

Figure 3

Fight in Progress

Puffy Padmore

Judges

Fighter B

Fighter A

The playground fighter on the left (*A*) is using his anorak as a matador's cape and yelling "Torro, Torro!" in an attempt to enrage his opponent into making an unwisely precipitant assault. So far the fighter on the right (*B*) has resisted the urge, preferring to do Dick Emery impressions to amuse the teenage girls who form one curve of the human ring. On the other side of the ring two of the judges are settling a disagreement over the legitimacy of an earlier Kwai Chang Caine by considered argument. Note the figure of "Puffy" Padmore approaching from the direction of the chemistry labs. His presence indicates that the fight is entering its closing stages.

Training

Like all combat sports, playground fighting is as much physical as psychological, for while it is important to have greater self-belief than your opponent it is usually much, much more important to be bigger and stronger than them. Often at the world's most prestigious events such as the Xtreme Playground Fighting Challenge we see fighters who are clearly much cleverer, calmer and more focused than their opposite number literally fold up physically. When it comes to playground fighting you should never underestimate the importance of brute force. Getting into fighting trim is, therefore, vital for any playground fighter.

DIET

Fresh fruit and vegetables, steamed fish and chicken, rice and spaghetti, you can forget all these. If the ordinary athlete's body is a temple then the playground fighter's body is a rather unsavoury amusement arcade down by the bus station. His diet must be built around the four core food groups: cheesy corn-based snacks, crisps, penny sweets and lurid green fizzy pop. On a typical pre-fight training day a top-class

Savoury *Sweet*

playground fighter such as Carl "Supermoose" Garbutt's menu would read something like this:

BREAKFAST – Smoky bacon crisps (well, he's not going to have roast chicken flavour for breakfast, is he?), quarter-of-a-pound of mixed penny selection including pink shrimps, black jacks, fruit salads and red laces, one quart of Texan Cream Soda.

LUNCH – Cheesy Wotsits, Quavers, salt and vinegar crisps, Twiglets, chipsticks, two Aztec bars, three Texan bars, a Curly Wurly, bag of American hardgums, a bottle of strawberry Cresta.

DINNER – A bag of chips and scraps followed by cheese sandwich biscuits, cheese footballs, Ritz crackers, tomato-sauce-flavoured crisps, a Topic bar (nuts removed and flicked at the dog), a Marathon bar (ditto), fresh selection of coconut mushrooms, cola bottles, hot lips, sherbet flying saucers and liquorice. One quart of dandelion and burdock.

BRITISH ASSOCIATION OF SCHOOLBOY HOOLIGANS

B.A.S.H.

The British Association of Schoolboy Hooligans (BASH) administers playground fighting in the UK. All major playground fighting events in England, Scotland and Wales take place under the governance of BASH (in Northern Ireland playground fighting is controlled by the H.M. Armed Forces), which also organises coaching courses and handles disciplinary matters. The highlight of the British playground fighting season is the BASH All-Britain Finals held round the back of the Empire Pool, Wembley on the first Saturday in November when there are no teachers about.

The beginner eager to get involved in scuffling at local and regional level should write to BASH for a list of his local clubs to the address below (remember to include a stamped addressed envelope, or we'll come round and pull your tie-knot so tight even your Mum won't be able to undo it for you).

I Am Looking For Trouble,
BASH, PO Box 25, London NW13 5BR

HEADLOCK

EST. 1997

For people who are serious about playground fighting

January 1974
5½p

Headlock (Est. 1907), is the only national periodical entirely devoted to the sport. Each issue is choc-a-bloc with interesting articles on a range of topics pertaining to playground fighting by people of whom you may have heard, tournament reports, equipment reviews, updates and developments and an amusing cartoon by resident artist "Twok".

"When I said gloves I didn't mean *boxing* gloves!!"

Subscriptions 66p (post paid)

tackle this sport **Playground Football**

Published with the assistance of the Scottish Society of Rush Goalies

U.K. PRICE
25p net
(Limp Cover Edition)

The Basics

Playground football, as the saying has it, "Is a stupid game played by stupid fellows".

The laws of the game are scant and if they have ever been written down then you can rest assured that no playground footballer worth his salt will ever have bothered reading them! Let us then take a very brief look at what is involved in this most subtle and fascinating of all sports.

THE BALL

In playground football it is vital that the ball conforms to regulations. These are that it must be either very old, or very cheap. Preferably both. The ideal ball for playground football is an ancient, leather caseball that has been fished out of the river by one of the boys and his dog earlier that morning. This ball is scarred and pitted like the face of a veteran bare-knuckle fighter, weighs the same as a bucket of tar and has laces that, when they smack bare skin, leave a livid weal like that left on the bodies of dead mariners by the poisonous tentacles of giant jellyfish. If no such ball can be fished from the river in time for the game then a good alternative is a bright orange plastic football bought from a garage on the way to the seaside. This is as light as meringue and, being not quite round, wobbles through the air like a wounded duck. It is more or less impossible to control, which is just as well as nobody likes a show-off.

Correct　　　　*Incorrect*

KIT

In ordinary football the players all wear boots. In playground football the rules are very different. Most of the players favour gym shoes, pumps, zip-up Chelsea boots with Cuban heels, or platform-soled monkey boots in silver with red lightening stripes. One of the most intriguing laws of the game makes it compulsory for at least one player on each team to wear Wellingtons.

According to the laws of the game a pair of fellows from each side must also wear belted gaberdine raincoats ("because me Mam says with my chest it's not worth risking getting a chill"). The wearing of an old leather flying helmet (for superpowered headers) is optional, but if taken must be worn only by a player who is also prepared to say "Bandits at 5 o'clock. Wilco Charlie. Let's blast 'em" and then make fighter plane noises including bombs and rockets.

Normally in football we expect to see the two teams wearing easily distinguished shirts. This is not the case in playground football where all the players are clad identically. If you want to know who is on your team you have to remember. And don't listen to that boy over there that is crying, "Away pass it to me, Terry man" over and over again. He is not on your team at all. He is a lying get.

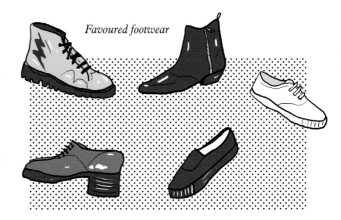

Favoured footwear

The Playing Area

Goalposts are usually jumpers, of course, while the exact position of the "bar" is generally determined by a long argument between the goalkeeper who reasons that "It went about a foot over me hands and I was jumping this high", and the player claiming the goal who counters, "No you weren't. You were leaning backwards and your elbows were bent, so you were more like this." Eventually after several minutes of fruitless discussion the matter is resolved by a wrestling match between the two (a knockout, two falls, or a submission to determine the winner. No kicking, bending fingers right back, or sticking chewing gum up your opponent's nostrils).

One touchline should be clearly demarcated by a wall, fence or the edge of the school playing field which is always too muddy for you to go on (or at least that's what the caretaker says, anyway), while the other should lie at a point so far away none of the players can be bothered to run after the ball once it has gone beyond it.

Bear in mind that at random moments during the game the dimensions of the pitch can be suddenly altered when: a game featuring younger players starts up in one corner; a gang of wayward boys turns up to practise smoking and spitting, or a pair of dinner ladies holding hands with lots of the little kids choose to stop in the centre circle and start playing pat-a-cake, pat-a-cake, baker's man.

The arrival of Puffy Padmore and his cycling proficiency test group with cones and several cardboard boxes designed to represent a parked car may also dramatically alter the size and shape of the playing area, especially since "a policeman will be coming along to carry out the test at some point and if the ball hits him woe betide the lot of you".

Remember: All people entering the playing area can be used for exciting moves such as ricochets and cannons. Playing a wall pass off a yard monitor is one of the game's most difficult skills to master.

A wonderfully deft toe-poke drops just under the bar. Or does it?

2.5 feet

Regulation goal size

Goals

LEGAL

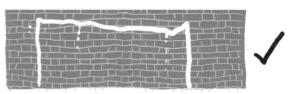

THE CLASSIC – Made from piles of jumpers, anoraks, caps and satchels. Both teams should check regularly for subsidence which may result in contraction of the size of the goal from the regulation "six big steps (no jumping) from a lad who is neither lanky nor titchy". This style of goal is popular with playground soccer purists but the lack of "rebounds" count against it in the eyes of many modern players.

THE WHITEWASH – Painted onto the wall of the school using some leftover paint from Uncle Bob's shed while Mr Sullen the caretaker was off sick with shingles. One of the few playground goals that has a bar (though it isn't very straight).

STICKS IN THE MUD – Goal is placed on the edge of the field, which is inevitably "too muddy for you bloody lot to go charging about on. You'll ruin the grass."

REFUSE – Using the playground litterbin as one post and a dustbin borrowed from round the back of Mr Sullen's sheds. The ball striking such posts makes a satisfying clang, which makes them the favourite of many playground football fans.

COOK'S – Goal is formed using the washing line post and clothes prop outside the kitchen. The clothesline acts as the bar, but since it is so thin as to be practically invisible it causes just as many disputes as the invisible version.

ILLEGAL

JUNIOR TICKS – Forming posts using two younger boys who are instructed to "stand right there and don't move or we'll knack you" is against the rules. Teams using such posts face a term-long ban from playground football, especially if it emerges that the goalkeeper has instructed to posts to "shuffle in a bit when they start to come up this end".

HAZARD – In this case one team has cunningly positioned the goal it is defending right in front of the science lab window in an attempt to deter the opposition from shooting. Such tactics are illegal and likely to end in both teams being made to stay behind after school and write five pages on the subject of "contrition".

Duration of the Game

The playground football match lasts from "after lunch" until "tea-time", a duration calculated by having a traditional British school cook boil a cabbage until it is cooked to her satisfaction – roughly four and a half hours. Half-time will occur when the two biggest lads are thirsty and will last as long as it takes for the puniest player to go to the shop and bring back bacon frazzlers, pop and a selection of flying saucers, liquorice laces and some of that sherbet that turns your tongue blue for the two teams.

The game ends when the cabbage has reached the consistency of pond slime and the cook appears at the edge of the playing surface yelling, "Your dinner's on the table. Come in this minute. I don't care if you are 3-2 down and just about to take a penalty. Your father didn't die in two World Wars so you could let good food go to waste. And stop that chuntering or I'll have the Playground Football Association suspend you for a fortnight without any pudding."

1st half

2nd half

Common Breaches of the Rules

(a) Kicking the ball with our toe "like a girl".

(b) Tripping opponent by kicking the bottom of his heel as he is running.

(c) Deliberately kicking the ball out of the playground to go and get a look at the rabbits "that bloke has on his allotment".

(d) Wearing open-toed sandals.

(e) Acting stupid just because you are losing.

(f) Affecting a bad limp after missing an open goal.

(g) Rolling round on the ground squealing like a big Jessie just because the ball hit you on your bare leg.

****

THE MOST IMPORTANT LAW OF ALL
Playground football is played to a strict code. The players are reminded that in the event of any dispute the decision of The Big Tough Boy Whose Brother Is In Borstal is final.

****

Selection

Before any game of playground football can begin the two teams have to be selected. This is done by the captains. The captains are traditionally the two best footballers in the playground. They stand together while the players available for selection line up against the wall looking either madly enthusiastic and muttering "Me, me, me!" and pointing at themselves, or arrogant and nonchalant, spitting on the floor and rubbing it in with the sole of their shoe, or fearful and spiritually crushed with a face the colour of sago.

The two captains then argue over who will get first pick. This is resolved by doing one-potato, two-potato, best of three. The selection process can now begin.

What follows is expertly described in *Playground Football – My Passport Round The Empire* by Archibald Farquarson-Grouse, one of the greatest players of the 1920s:

"*There is probably not a chap the length and breadth of this great country of ours that has not experienced the tremendous highs and loathsome lows of the 'picking process'. First the awful optimism as a captain's finger seems about to point in your direction, only suddenly to divert away to a ginger-haired lout with a powerful right-foot and a half-pound bag of pineapple cubes (a sweet incidentally which, by dint of its angular shape and sugar coating, exquisitely combined pleasure and pain, filling your mouth with delicious flavours while simultaneously scraping the skin off your tongue).*

"*Then the feeling of dread abandonment as the fellows around you gradually dwindle until there were more lined up behind the skippers than there are standing against the wall. The whole odious spectacle exacerbated by the captains' habit of engaging in noisy debate over the merits of those that are left: 'I'm not having him. He kicks like a girl.' 'Yeah, but at least he kicks. That one's only ever got one goal and that was when it bounced in off his belly.'*

"*And on it would go through its inevitable and grisly phases: the horrible realisation that you were the oldest player left, that they were picking little kids ahead of*

The captains make their selections. The skipper on the right is attempting to seal a "If I have Nosher, you can have fatso and the speccy get" deal with his opposite number.

you. The jump in your heart as one team leader raised his head and said, 'All right, I'll have lanky' only for your stomach to sink as your eager step forward was greeted with a terse, 'No, not you, lanky. That lanky.' And finally with just three players left the divvying up: 'I'll take the tubby lad with asthma, you can have the other pair'.

"Not, I should add that I ever suffered in such a manner. It wasn't my football skills that saved me, though. It was because from early on I realised that if I turned up with a quart bottle of lurid green fizzy pop and held it in front of my chest I'd usually get selected shortly after all the genuine talent had gone".

At international level the system is somewhat different, of course. The Federation International de Football de Cour de Recreation (FIFCR) operates a rankings system that mimics the popular "You get two of the little kids and we'll have our Gary" system. Under these rankings an established star is the equivalent of 1.5 ordinary members of an international squad, or a dozen non-international-

Comical dribbling is an effective tactic against a massed defence

ists. This system has led to greater tactical flexibility for coaches as they weigh up the possibilities of selecting the best available players and using a 4-4-2 system or opting instead to give mediocrity a chance in a 12-12-28 formation. It also allows a good player to show off a bit more by dribbling round whole teams of rubbish 'uns, sometimes while doing a Norman Wisdom impression, or using only his weaker foot.

A Game in Progress

Dinner lady
(with cup of tea)

Girls playing
elastic skips

Metalwork
teachers motorbike
and sidecar

Tufty the Squirrel –
road safety obsessed
rodent

Cones from cycling
proficiency test

The Positions

A rush goalie attempts to get back into position. Running backwards provides a better view of play, but can result in a nasty accident with a skipping rope, or milk trolley

Playground football may, to the untutored eye, resemble nothing more than a free-for-all in which kids simply kick the ball and then everybody runs after it screaming, but nothing could be further from the truth.

RUSH GOALIE

The rush goalie is a goalkeeper of proven footballing ability (or better still a footballer of proven goalkeeping ability) with licence to rove about the field as he sees fit. The rush goalie adds flexibility to any team, allowing managers to switch forma-

tions effortlessly from 1-2-17 to 2-2-17, 1-2-18 or even a continental-style 1-3-17. At times the rush goalie may be caught out of position and way up field when the opposition break away after a corner or prolonged scuffle when the ball has got stuck in a drain hole over by the school secretary's office. In this case he can either race back as fast as he can making a noise like a fire engine siren, or alternately one of his team mates can institute the "change of goalies" rule, which allows anyone to take over between the sticks, so long as they are wearing gloves.

A typical hogger in action – spectacular, yet often unproductive

THE HOGGER

A key component of any playground football team (indeed most line-ups feature at least six), the hogger's role is simplicity itself: he gets the ball and dribbles past opponent after opponent, then turns round and dribbles past them again. While dribbling he is totally oblivious to kicks, trips, dead legs, punches on the arm and attempts to break his mesmerising spell over the football by offering him bags of sherbet flying saucers, or claiming that a woman in the window of a house opposite is stood there in her bra, honest. He is also totally deaf to his team mates who are lined up in front of goal unmarked and yelling, "Pass it here! Pass it here! Away and pass it, man, you ball greedy nit!" Capable of retaining possession for twenty minutes at a stretch unless distracted by the sound of an ice-cream van or Mrs Garbutt grabbing him by the ear and dragging him in to class to complete his maths homework, the hogger is particularly useful in away ties in Europe, or when defending a 12–11 lead with just thirty minutes remaining.

A goal hanger celebrates a two-yard deflecting heel-nudge in flamboyant "Apeman" style

THE GOAL HANGER

A totally different animal to the goal scrounger (who loiters about the penalty box in the hope of deflecting in somebody else's shot), the goal hanger literally hangs around in the opposition goalmouth, distracting the keeper by reciting bits from *The Dick Emery Show*, getting him to do his impression of Harry Worth and begging to have a go with his gloves in exchange for a swig of Lucozade and bubblegum cards of *Land of the Giants*. When the ball comes his way, however, the hanger is lightning quick, slotting it coolly home and then doing an elaborate Tarzan-style goal celebration involving a loud "jungle call", chimp imitation and shouts of "Unk Tantor!" The celebration expends far more energy than he does during the game.

A little kid uses his diminutive stature to unsettle a much larger opponent. Remember: a flea may irritate an elephant!

LITTLE KID

Little Kid uses his small stature to create mayhem by peskily jogging alongside bigger opponents, poking them in the ribs and saying things like "What's the weather like up there?" and "Watch out, or I'll bite your kneecaps". At set plays Little Kid is traditionally carried into the penalty area on his tallest team mate's shoulders where he unsettles the opposing goalkeeper, usually by grabbing his cap and throwing it into a puddle.

CRAZY KID

Crazy Kid is basically Little Kid after he has drunk a quart bottle of Texan Cream Soda and eaten a half-pound bag of rhubard-and-custards. Fired up with sugar he hurtles wildly about the pitch yelling, "I'm crazy man, me, woohoo!" tackling everyone including his own team mates and booting the ball as hard as he can in whatever direction he happens to be facing. The Crazy Kid is a useful weapon if a team needs to break up the pattern of play and disrupt the opposition, who often become totally demoralised by his antics and threaten to leave the field unless "he stops acting mental and plays properly".

The Big Carl in action – seldom pretty, but so hard to defend against!

BIG CARL

Big Carl is the role taken by the very large boy who is not fat but just big-boned, or probably it is just some sort of medical thing, because he is very hard indeed and it is best not to upset him, really. Due to his immense girth the Big Carl is not very mobile, however he forms a formidable defensive barrier, partly because he is so huge, but mainly because he is armed with a catapult and pocketful of marbles. When he was younger the Big Carl was generally forced to go in goal by the older boys. This has left him with a particular hatred for all custodians and at set pieces he is often designated to mark them – usually by embossing their forehead with his signet ring.

BABY BROTHER

Not to be confused with Little Kid, Baby Brother is only there because "Our Mam said I had to bring him with us". Baby Brother traditionally rejects normal shoes in favour of a pair of old wellies that are three sizes too big for him. This means that when he kicks the ball his welly flies off after it, bemusing goalkeepers and causing defenders to dive for cover – a penalty technique that often pays dividends. Some teams favour using a whole gang of baby brothers in a mass "7th Cavalry defence". (*See formations over*)

The Formations

SYSTEM: 1-17-1

The classic English formation favoured on these shores for more than a century. The crowded midfield springs forward en masse when the lone defender, or goalie hoofs the ball down the field with a cry of "Three points to Wigan", and rushes in pursuit of the ball, while the designated goal scrounger stands near the opposition goal trying to look innocent. Recently the inflexibility of the system, which often sees 90 per cent of the team crowded in the top left-hand corner of the pitch, was exposed by "foreigners" who exploited the resulting space on the rest of the field using a clearly underhand, but apparently legal, tactic known as "passing".

SYSTEM: 4-12-0

A largely defensive formation with just one man designated to break up field after long balls pumped out of defence by the goalie. As you can see the lone "breaker" is mounted on a bicycle with "cowhorn" handlebars. This gives him greater speed and mobility, while the fact that the brakes don't work very well, and the protruding front light is strategically placed at groin level, make him hard to handle even for the most rugged central defenders. Tactically astute teams will counteract the lone frontman simply by man-marking him, or sticking a broom handle through his spokes.

SYSTEM: 1-2-17

A variation on the classic English system. In this case the defender operates as the glamorous continental style "libero" and is given licence to roam all over the pitch sometimes even crossing right over the yard in the hope of persuading one of the girls sitting on the wall reading *Jackie* to show him her pants. Often the prospect that she might just do it is enough to distract the opposition from all thoughts of attacking endeavour and instead stroll around with their mouths hanging open trying to look like they're not that excited about the idea, or anything.

SYSTEM: 7-2-10

A system often employed by teams forced to field a large number of Little Kids or Baby Brothers (*see Players*) is the popular "7th Cavalry defence". In this a large group of smaller players gather in the goalmouth where they observe play. When an opposition player approaches with the ball one of the group makes the sound of a bugle call, another yells, "Troop, yoah!" in a John Wayne voice and the whole bunch charge forward, surrounding the opponent. Maddened by the swarm of diminutive defenders with their whoops and kicks he soon loses possession and once the ball has been hacked up field the defensive group returns to the goalmouth to swap new swearwords and discuss last night's episode of *The Wacky Races*.

A must-read for anybody that wants to understand the laws of Playground Football

YOU Are The Big Tough Boy Whose Brother Is In Borstal!

A desperate clearance out of St Cuthbert's defence...

strikes the right calf of a girl playing with clackers...

and rebounds into the path of Puffy Padmore who is advancing to quell a playground scrap near the coal heap...

the ball rolls in front of his striding leg and is inadvertently walloped past the goalkeeper of Lord St John Stevas Secondary Modern.

Now available as a fully black-and-white softback from BCP publishing. Available from all good sports shops, booksellers and the better sort of provincial newsagent

DO YOU?

Award a drop ball next to the clackers lass.

Signal a goal by yelling, "Get in there, Puffy!"

Grab the nearest little kid and give him a painful Chinese burn.

Only you can decide. You are the big tough boy whose brother is in borstal!

Xtreme Playground

...oduced in association with WOWSA,
... World Organisation Of Unconventionally Spelled Activities

U.K. PRICE **65p net**

Para-Shorting

Para-shorting, or hang-panting as it is sometimes known, is one of the most exciting, dangerous, spectacular and, yes, xtreme of all Xtreme sports. Nobody witnessing the graceful ascent and acrobatic aeronautics of the top-class competitor with a full thermal gust in the legs of his flying shorts could fail to be impressed, though only the bravest of the brave will want to give it a try themselves. As World Champion Sigurd Kroch of Iceland famously said, "I fly these pants, so the rest of you don't have to."

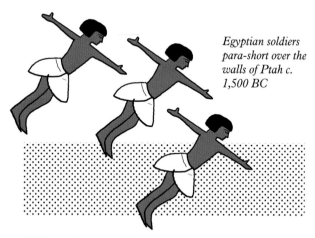

Egyptian soldiers para-short over the walls of Ptah c. 1,500 BC

ORIGINS

There are references to para-shorting going all the way back to Ancient Egypt where hieroglyphics on the tomb of Tutankhamen clearly show soldiers flying over the walls of besieged cities using the up-draught of wind blowing up their cotton kilts. In China during the Hang Dynasty the Emperor's concubines commonly wore kite-girdles and the sight of these beautiful ladies circling over the For-bidden Quarter of Beijing convinced the population of the Divinity of the Celestial Kingdom.

The Maoris, Turcomans, the Pygmies of the Cameroon and a number of other native peoples also have their own traditions of air-powered lower-garment related sports, but the event most westerners know and love from the brief glimpses they have caught of it on *World of Sport* when Dickie Davies has nothing better to fill up the time between the racing and the wrestling really began life in the mountains of Switzerland. Here the pursuit of lederhose-leaping (or Alpine Fol-de-rol – literally "break the wind and tumble" – as it is called in Helvetian) first became popular in the eighteenth century amongst lonely goatherds and wandering bankers.

By Victorian times villagers all across the cantons were harnessing the elevating powers of wind and leather to engage in jumping contests that, with the Mistral, or a phalanx of Alpine horns at their backs, could see the leapers clear a line of 24 yodellers in a single amazing bound. The sport quickly spread through the rest of the Alpine nations and soon had many regional variations including one aimed specifically at women, Bavarian Dirndlhoppe. Novelist Arthur Conan Doyle was the man who first brought the sport to Britain and it even features in one of his Sherlock Holmes stories, "The Case of the Rickmansworth Leg".

At the first Winter Olympiad held in 1924 both men and women's fol-de-rol was very much on the agenda. Unfortunately the sport was subsequently

Traditional leather shorts are still used for Alpine Fol-de-rol to this day

dropped thanks to the intervention of puritanical US Olympic commissioner Savery Grudge who claimed that the only reason it was so popular was because "it afforded the public ample opportunity to stare up young ladies' skirts". Thankfully these days, thanks to the efforts of the likes of Hugh Hefner, Harold Robbins and Germaine Greer, such repressive attitudes to the perfectly normal and natural desire to stare at women's knickers while pretending to be interested in something else entirely are very much a thing of the past. As a result Fol-de-rol may yet make a reappearance on Olympic pistes in the 1980s.

Para-Shorting Today

Things have certainly steamed a long way down the lonesome highway marked Existential Fulfilment since the time when Count Adelman von Chuff of Austria claimed Olympic gold with a 58-second schutztutenfruten with Sylvia Krstel dismount. In fact, amongst today's para-shorters such minimal airtime would probably earn a big razza, rather than the chorus of riffing yet non-aggressive AOR from Toto, Kansas or REO Speedwagon that greets the star performers of today.

Superior fitness, better diet (gone are the pre-competition repasts of lobster, ox-tongue and chilled hock and in have come scientifically approved meals of baked beans and Texan cream soda) and, most importantly, fantastic new hi-performance equipment from ace manufacturers such as Schmuck, Pock-Muppet and Slap Ape, who reject the commonplace commercialism of most sportswear makers in favour of selling large amounts of stuff to kids at very high prices. As a consequence of the input of the world's greatest para-shorters

A Hawaiian para-shorter performs a "Big chopper". Note his ripstop Bermudas with aerodynamic windgrip whirls.

(OK the guys get paid, but that's the system, right? They didn't invent it, they just live in it) the gear has gone stratospheric, in every sense of the word. In place of lederhosen or tweed plus-fours today's "shorters" wear immense, billowing para-shorts fashioned from manmade fibres developed during Richard Nixon's famous "War on Commies in Outer Space" programme.

On the beaches of California and Hawaii – where the sport literally took off in the 1960s spawning its own distinctive cultural scene, perhaps most evocatively captured by the shorting music of Pearl & Dean and The Wind Brothers – shorters harness the sea breezes to ascend to heights of over 100 yards, carried heavenwards purely by their aerodynamic big-pants.

While in the air top-class performers quickly learned to carry out complicated acrobatic manoeuvres which are marked by a panel of expert judges for "difficulty", "execution" and "like total, you know, far-outness". Cornish teenager Lancelot Phlange, one of a new breed of UK para-shorters who seem certain to threaten to probably get close to breaking into the world's top 300 in all likelihood at some point in the future but not immediately obviously because we just don't have the facilities or the funding in the UK says, "The sport gives you an incredible buzz. It is just you, up there in the wind, wrestling to keep your shorts under control."

Worries have been expressed amongst some establishment figures about the dangers of the sport because of the large number of injuries sus-

Sudden wind seepage is an ever present danger!

tained as a result of "gusset drop" – the sudden escape of air through weakened seams that can cause shorters to plummet to earth at high speeds. Shorters like Phlange, however, love risk and are dismissive of the perils involved in their sport. "OK, things sometimes go wrong," he has said. "Every once in a while some guy drops out of the sky and lands on an old lady out walking her dog. But accidents happen. She could just as easily have been crushed under the wheels of a speeding juggernaut, or had a cake explode in her face."

A Typical Para-Shorter

The para-shorter is wearing TC Cakehole™ gustothene™ knee-length krazy-wilf-batik™ megapants™ with 48-inch hems, giving him a short capacity of 37 cubic feet, just about the maximum number of "cubies" a solo para-shorter can control. Generally over 40ft ^{3} will lead to a shorter "busting his stays" and flying off into outer space. (Larger shorts are available, but are usually only used for pairs shorting events. Going tandem is a good way for the beginner to learn, so long as he can persuade an experienced performer to share shorts with him/her.)

His harness is worn over-shoulder style and attached to a 6-inch piton, which has been cemented into a large rock using Plasticene™ to limit the chances of him "ripping peg" and being blown hundreds of miles away. Piston™ wristbands and headband, Skab™ sneakers and a vest bearing a powerful anti-establishment message "I Leave All The Lights On In My Bedroom Even When I'm Downstairs" complete the ensemble. Radical!

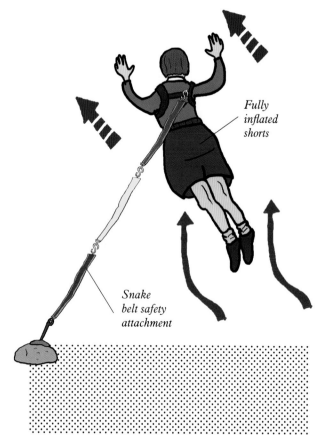

Fully inflated shorts

Snake belt safety attachment

Para-Shorting Moves

"Throwing a Big Tosser"
(a) Shorter pulls a cheesy-toe
(b) Eases into a triple Zapata
(c) Finishes with a series of
    underarm hobbits

"Grabbing Free Mints"
(a) Shorter crushes the chunks
(b) Seamlessly moves into an
    overhead lamp
(c) Performs an upside-down
    Sacha
(d) Lands Slavic-style

"Busting Crabs"
(a) Shorter goes sloth
(b) Performs a couple of
    Laverne and Shirleys
(c) Executes the Nedwell
    slump

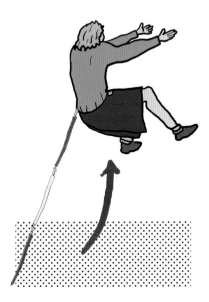

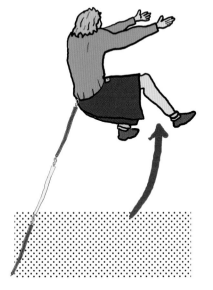

"Tartan Hurl"
(a) Shorter enters freefall
    plummet with goose-waggle
(b) Up-swoops Stranks-fashion
(c) Does the do
(d) Gives it the big drooper
(e) F-Troop landing

"Holding the Little Horse"
(a) Shorter starts with a
    sequence of simple 98ers
(b) Racks up a big pie
(c) Turns dirty-side up
(d) Disengages like a
    Dutchman

"Riding the Purple Turtle"
(a) Shorter hangs his hems
(b) Chucks a sly and squeaky
(c) Makes like Albie Keane
(d) Finishes with a triple
    word score

Micro-Shorting

Despite its name this latest off-shoot of the power-shorting scene does not feature hotpants! Micro-shorting is a self-powered para-shorting experience for those who want new high-altitude thrills even at times when there is no breeze to speak of. Micro-shorts have all the features of para-shorts but with the addition of a small motor – usually liberated from Dad's lawnmower – that drives a plastic propeller. The power unit is fitted to the belt loops of the shorts with the prop forcing air both downwards to give uplift and into the legs of the shorts for extra buoyancy. Using just a gallon of two-stroke (stored in a tank tucked into the shorters headband) heights of up to 1,500 feet and distances of over 100 miles can be attained. In 1976 the British Government at the behest of the military, attempted to ban micro-shorting after a German micro-shorter drifted across the North Sea, triggering a nuclear alert. The incident was recently celebrated in the hit single "Neun und Neunzig Luftenhosen" by a German lady with hairy armpits.

Fuel-tank headband

Motor

A microshorter in full kit prepares for liftoff!

Butt-luge

Low-cost thrills is the name of the game with this rapidly growing sport in which contestants dispense with equipment altogether and simply slide down a hill on their backsides.

ORIGINS

Butt-luging developed during medieval times, evolving from Gloucestershire's cheese-rolling tradition and the popular Herefordshire sport of downhill whey-chasing. It is a fact little known in Britain today that cheese was not initially eaten at all, but used only for rural leisure activities such as the above, Wensleydale Pigknock, Tossing the Truckle, Mendip Butterslut etc. (*see Tackle This Sport no.787* Yokel Dairy Product Games of Old England *for more details*). It was not until the Huguenots arrived from France in the 17th century that cheese found its way onto the English dining table, and even then for more than a century it was served with cherry pie-filling and custard as a pudding!

The Pilgrim Hayseeds who set off from Bristol in 1627 in their ship The Owd Sow carried traditional cheese games to the New World. Sadly the early American settlers found local buffalo and antelope milk could be used only for making creamy cheese like the modern Philadelphia. This was highly unsuitable for hill rolling or chasing as it tended to stick in the grass. The lack of a traditional rugged English rolling cheese initially seemed to preclude a madcap dash down a precipitous slope, until a man whose name has come down to us only as "That Madbugger Bernard" came up with the solution, dispensing with the cheese altogether and simply sliding down a hill on the seat of your pants for the sheer thrill of the thing. So was born butt-luge, or as it was known in those more puritanical times, upper-leg sledging.

BUTT-LUGING TODAY

Since those early times butt-luging has gone from strength to strength not least because of the invention of denim, which remains the official sliding fabric of the Federation International de Federation National De Cou Glissant, the sport's governing body, to this day.

Note feet are "in the stirrups" to increase speed and stop soil getting up his trousers

Since the 1960s butt-luge competitions have sprung up around the world and many of the more socially conscious cities and towns around the UK and Europe have even built special urban butt-luge courses so youngsters have somewhere to go and hover around smoking, stamping on cans, imitating peacock calls and yelling abuse at passing vicars. A new variant of the sport, beach butt-luge, is also proving highly popular.

At its most simple butt-luge may look like nothing more than a person sliding down a hill on their bottoms. However, anybody who has attended an event such as the Malvern Hills Open, or the Garmisch-Partenkirchen Arschslus will know different. At these top-class competitions lugers in specially polished jeans weave in and out of the gorse bushes at speeds of up to 75mph, frequently leap twenty or more feet in the air, and sometimes suffer severe bracken and heather-related injuries.

World Champion Mike "Mudchute" Malone of Colorado says, "Sure there are big risks associated with butt-luge, I mean, like, you can get grass burns, your undershorts can get pulled way up your ass causing painful chaffing and your Mom is likely to go crazy when she sees the green stains on the back of your Wranglers, but what is life without risk? Shit happens. But that was just once and it was years ago, so there's no need to keep chanting, 'Mikey filled his dipey' every time I appear, is there? Come on, fellas, give me a break, willya."

A BUTT-LUGE COMPETITION

Our illustration shows a typical Regional B-Grade Butt-Luge Competition in which a dozen lugers are racing down a hillside in Cumbria. Competitor A has taken an early lead having correctly judged the line around a large clump of blackberry bushes. Competitor B has "gone woolly", while Competitor C has lost control and been flipped over onto his front (known as "yanking raw nipple"). If he does not manage to right himself quickly he may suffer severe T-shirt ride-up. Competitor D has hit a cowpat and become becalmed. He will be lucky to finish, or to get a lift home afterwards. Note the judges standing to the right of the slope. They are there to watch for infringements such as the tucking of copies of *Titbits* down the back of the trousers, or the use of performance-enhancing slugs, the slime of which is sometimes illegally rubbed onto the seat of their pants by cheating foreigners.

GBH Biking

The riders have decided not to use bicycle clips and may suffer "flare-in-the-chain" problems as a consequence

A new discipline from the urban centres of the UK that grew out of BMX-ing, GBH-ing is a thrilling combination of bike-born mayhem and playground fighting that calls to mind the medieval joust. Riders pedal towards each other at breakneck speed and collide in a whirl of mudguards, bells and string-bags filled with stuff their mother sent them to the shops for. Raw indeed!

"The subtle difference between BMX and GBH," says Nosher Davies of the British GBH Federation, "is that with your traditional BMX you perform on the half-pipe whereas in GBH-ing it's more the windpipe. Hurgh, hurgh, hurgh! Or at least that's what we like to say for a catchy phrase. Because obviously it's not actually as violent as all that. But you mustn't let on to the kids, or they'll stop coming. It's like karate. Once they discover you aren't going to teach them how to decapitate someone with a single blow, they all bugger off to watch a Bruce Lee film."

According to Davies, who runs his own GBH-ing centre in Bermondsey, the sport grew out of a disenchantment with cultural aspects of the Xtreme scene. "Many working-class, inner-city kids were bored by the whole co-operative, non-competitive, scruffy, bourgeois, snivelling wimp element involved in other Xtreme playground events."

In contrast to the baggy fashions favoured by most Xtremers the GBH crowd favour a straighter look of nicely ironed, clean, white shirts, neatly knotted ties, box-fresh blazers and grey flannel trousers with razor-sharp creases down the fronts, "Basically," Davies explains, "it's a look that says, 'I live at home with my Mum. What are you going to do about it?'"

A TYPICAL GBH-ER

The rider is mounted on a traditional "get-off-and-milk-it" cycle found in his grandmother's outhouse. He has replaced the handlebars with "cowhorns" for the fashionable speedway look and will twist the grips as if they were throttles before setting off. His weaponry includes a shield and lance and a loud horn. Added cover is provided by the frontal basket that contains two pounds of beetroots old Mr Bobbins down the allotments asked him to pass on to his Mum. These maybe deployed as "hand grenades" during the competition. Note the colander attached to his ears with rubber bands. Such protective headgear is compulsory for GBH biking competitions in the UK.

'Cowhorn' handlebar

Dustbin lid shield

Colander helmet

Yard-brush lance

Basket

Sprung seat saddle

69

GBH Biking Competitions

The person whose feet first touch the ground is the loser

A tandem tournament. Double the numbers, double the fun!

HIGH NOON

The sort of GBH-biking tournament you will come across in schoolyards on Saturday afternoons. The High Noon is a simple boy-to-boy duel. The riders stare at one another for several minutes before one yells, "Go for your gun, mister!" at which point they both ride towards one another and a brutal contest for ascendancy begins. Note that one rider is armed with traditional broom and dustbin lid while the other has opted to go "Tonto-style".

CAN YOU RIDE TANDEM?

Named in honour of the popular phrase from the PG Tips tea advert. Follows the same format as High Noon but in this case the rider is giving a passenger a croggy (he sits on the seat, while the rider stands on the pedals). Note that both croggies carry a flapping jumper. They will attempt to throw this so that it wraps around the face of the opposing rider, temporarily blinding him and causing him to crash into the girl's outside toilet.

A spectacular Evel Knievel end to the tournament!

Rider A

OK CORRAL

Arguably the most spectacular of all GBH-ing events, this one sees two teams of riders circling round and round the playing area while attempting to lasso one another with lengths of washing line. This could be xtremely dangerous if successful, but luckily it never is. Note that Rider A has dispensed with the washing line lasso in favour of a set of Gaucho-style bolas made from a pair of clackers.

THE CLOSING CEREMONY

Traditionally at the end of the contest defeated riders are asked to lie side-by-side on the ground while the winners make a ramp using six bricks and an old shed door and attempt to leap over them. The judges meanwhile retire to a position behind the bikeshed to prepare a report on the event that will be filed with the British GBH Federation and used in compiling the national rankings.

How To Get Involved In Xtreme Playground

The new pamphlet issued by HM Government Ministry of Sport and entitled "You Can Say What You Like About The Younger Generation, But You Certainly Have To Admire Their Energy" has lots of useful addresses for the would-be xtremist, but for those seeking the authentic, uncooked reality nothing beats the thriving street scene.

Para-shorting – There are dedicated para-shorting sites in Snowdonia, the Peak District, the North Pennines and North York Moors. There are also cliff-shorting centres in Cornwall and Kent. During the winter, when high winds make outdoor shorting hazardous, a number of venues host indoor shorting events in which lift is created by hundreds of household fans. The biggest such event is held at RAF Orpington in December with para-shorters frequently going straight through the roof of number one hanger on gusts provided by the engines of Phantom jets.

Butt-Luge – Britain's biggest butt-luge festival is held in Glastonbury, Somerset every summer. However many younger and more radical butt-lugers feel this has recently been hi-jacked by middle-class bourgeois weekend butt-lugers who have brought cavalry twills and corduroy to the slopes. For more "out there" butt-luge events visit your local high-street jeans emporium and ask the girl behind the counter with the mauve eye-shadow if she knows where it's at.

GBH Biking – Merseyside, the East End of Glasgow, Teesside and South-East London all have thriving GBH-ing scenes. To find out what is going on in your area simply consult one of the boys who hangs around outside the off-licence spitting on the pavement and rubbing it in with his foot.

Street Tuffet – Officially Britain's fastest-growing xtreme sport, street tuffet clubs can now be found in most towns in the UK. Your local leisure centre is a good place to start, many run beginners street tuffet courses at the indoor bowling green on Thursday mornings when the bowlers are queuing up in the post office for their pensions.

Playground Winter Games

TSP tackle
this sport

Association With The Anglo-Swiss Mittens-On-Elastic Club

U.K. PRICE **35p net**

Background

The winter playground is purely and simply one of the world's great sporting environments, with dozens of exciting activities taking place all over the snow and ice. We'll deal with the individual events later, but to give you some idea of just what is on offer here is an artist's impression of Middlecastle Primary School Playground at morning break one cold day in early February.

WINTER WONDERLAND – Sporters are in action all over the playground. We can see sliders, rollers and ballers in action, while a group of boys are completing the final leg of the council-sign biathlon. The mound of snow in the centre of the playground marks where some older sporters have buried that boy from class one who does Scottish dancing and plays laggy skips with the girls. Although cold he is in no danger just so long as someone digs him out before nightfall, and in actual fact the experience may toughen him up a bit, which will be for the best in the long run. Note that one old-age pensioner has diverted her normal route to the post office especially so that she can complain that she could have fallen on one of the slides and broken her hip. She has taken her complaint to Mr Sullen the caretaker and he has readily agreed to destroy the slide using boiling water and a handful of gravel because it is "a right bloody hazard and to tell you the truth, Mrs Johnson, if I'd known what this country was going to end up like what with the permissive society, *Play for Today* and bloomin' Simon Dee, I'd not have bothered losing my pancreas to the Africa Korps, I can tell you". In response some of the sliders are scratching a protest into the frost on the window of Puffy Padmore's classroom. A demand for freedom and tolerance for sliders everywhere, it reads, "Sullin Iz A Big Nancy. True."

To complete the scene a pair of older girls stand staring into space, imagining they are drinking hot wine with dreamy French ski ace Jean-Claude Killy.

Old age pensioner

Caretaker

Council-sign bi-athlete

Sullin Iz
A Big Nancy
True

Words
written
in frost

Rollers

Sliders

Ballers

What to Wear on Slope and Slide

When entering the glamorous and fun world of the winter playground it is vital that you have the right clothing and equipment. This diagram of a fully-kitted-out winter-sporter shows everything that you will need.

THE CORRECT KIT – Note the hand-knitted balaclava traditionally made from lots of lengths of wool his granny had left over from doing the jumpers for our Maureen's new twins. The lower part of the balaclava is usually worn up over the mouth so that after prolonged activity it becomes damp with condensation and then freezes to the lower lip re-

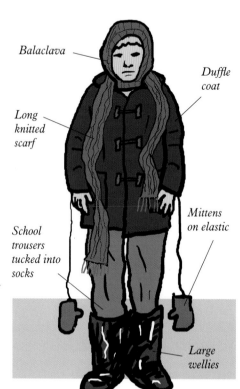

Balaclava

Duffle coat

Long knitted scarf

School trousers tucked into socks

Mittens on elastic

Large wellies

sulting in a nice sore. The duffle coat traditionally has the hood up for added warmth and prevent rivals from filling it full of snow. This experienced sporter has opted to tuck his trousers into his socks, which prevents the socks sliding inside the Wellington, something that can result in painful chafing to the calves. The woollen mittens are worn attached to elastic. This may well look a bit babyish but you have lost two pairs already this term, my lad, and money doesn't grow on trees, you know. Well, frankly, I don't care what Carl Spriggett says. He is not paying for new gloves every five minutes, is he?

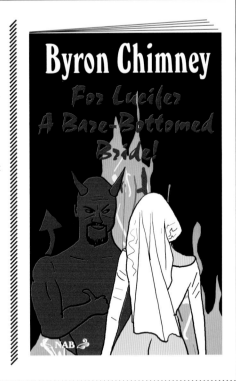

Sliding

The sport of sliding (or bi-pedal para-linear shoe-blading as it is known in the USA) was first recorded in Britain by Julius Caesar. Later Queen Boudicca of the Iceni almost brought an end to Roman rule in Britain when she made an entire Legion fall over on a whopping great slide she and her tribesmen had secretly prepared near Colchester. Through the judicious use of salt the Governor of Britannia, Marcus Fabius, eventually put an end to the Celtic threat, but the British Isles' reputation as the epicentre of world sliding remains. The expression "Britain is sliding fast" is heard everywhere you go these days, and no wonder!

GETTING STARTED IN SLIDING

The slider's equipment is very simple. He will need to don similar clothing to the winter sporter shown previously with one important difference: he must wear normal shoes not Wellingtons. Wellingtons have rubber soles and rubber soles make sliding impossible. The best shoes for sliding have leather soles. The authorities (i.e. your Mum) are remarkably reluctant to let you wear your best shoes out on a day when there is snow on the ground claiming that, "if they get wet it will ruin them with water marks". Luckily most schools will not let you wear wellies in the classroom, or assembly hall, and so you will have to take your proper shoes to school in that girly little cloth bag your Aunt Nelly made out of blue gingham and decorated with an embroidered picture of Andy Pandy "because he was always your favourite when you were a bairn". Carrying this will lead to other boys teasing you with cries of "Oooh, love the handbag, dahling" and suchlike. It is just as well the bag has a very long draw string which means you can swing it round like a mace and clock them in the mush with it, or things might get out of hand (*See* Tackle This Sport – Playground Fighting *for further details on the use of school bags in combat situations*). Once at school you can put your proper shoes on and keep them on for the rest of the day. Sliding may now commence.

Correct

Incorrect

MAKING A SLIDE

Making a slide is simple, but like all simple things there is an art to it. First of all select a strip of the playground that is flat or slopes slightly downhill. If it runs right outside a door or across a blind corner so much the better. It will also have to have sufficient space at both ends for a run-up and a stop zone. The latter is very important

A CORRECTLY SITED SLIDE – The illustration above shows a correctly located slide. There is a ten-pace run-up and several yards at the end of

the piste to allow the sliders to slow down before halting. Note the dustbins. These can be brought into play for a "comedy" finish.

Once you have located a site, you and at least four other sliders will have to get to work creating the piste by flattening it, spitting on it and then gradually working up a glossy sheen by shuffling on it ice-skater style. Never attempt this on your own.

Remember: It takes more than one pair of feet to make a slide.

A distance slider adopts the aerodynamic "piste" position. Note how the balaclava and hood make him more streamlined

Sliding events can be divided into two categories:

DISTANCE SLIDING

The simplest and most dynamic of the sliding disciplines, distance sliding (or DS) as its name implies is all about who slides the furthest. Sliders must all commence at the same line, no secondary sliding is allowed after a slider has come to a halt, all distances to be measured by the Big Tough Boy Whose Brother Is In Borstal using big steps.

ARTISTIC SLIDING

Very much a breathtaking fusion of speed and grace, artistic sliding sees shoe-bladers attempting to impress a panel of judges made up of the Big Tough Boy Whose Brother Is In Borstal and anybody else who doesn't mind him eating all their Jelly Tots. Sliders run up and set off from the mark sliding along the piste while executing a series of complex and difficult manoeuvres, a few of which are illustrated right:

1. Try to co-ordinate kick and yell

2. Doing a Wisdom – always a crowd pleaser

3. A tight jersey adds comedic value

THE COSSACK

Inspired by the appearance on ITV of the Tony Curtis and Yul Brynner classic *Taras Bulba*. Slider folds his arms, sticks one leg out, drops into a crouch, then bounces up and down yelling "Hah!" (*figure 1*)

THE LAUREL & HARDY

In homage to the great comedy duo the slider whirls his arms around as if about to fall over while going "Oah-ho-whoaaaaaaaah!" An interesting variation is the Mr Grimsdale, in which the slider performs a similar manoeuvre but with his school cap on back to front. (*figure 2*)

THE LITTLE WOMAN

Arguably the most famous of all artistic sliding moves, this old classic sees the competitor discard his coat before the performance. He then begins his slide, drops into a crouch and pulls his jumper over his knees to give the impression of a pint-sized lady with a large bosom. (*figure 3*)

Marks are awarded for difficulty, artistic impression and the ability to swerve round recumbent old folk, yellow pools of dog pee and birdcage grit sprinkled by Puffy Padmore because "Mrs Gamm the dinner lady could measure her length on this".

Sledge-standing

Sledge-standing, or ss-tanding as it is known to it's adherents, was invented in Yorkshire in the early sixties by kids who wanted something that reflected their eco-friendly lifestyles more fully than the then highly popular but deeply commercialised world of poly-bagging (sliding down a snow-covered hill while sitting on a fertiliser sack).

"Every poly-bag comes with, like, the name of some massive agro-chemical company written all over it," pioneering ss-tander Carl Smith of Whitby observed in 1968 "It's a total commercial sell-out. And besides, sometimes the farmers put cow shite in them and stuff."

Rejecting the poly-bags, these radical youngsters took to standing up on old-fashioned wooden toboggans (known as "woodies") and clutching the string like the reins of a horse. They quickly discovered that by yanking their woodies from side to side they could take them through a complicated series of wild acrobatic manoeuvres.

1. Good foot placement is essential

2. An excellent starting position for the novice

THE LESTER PIGGOT
Stander heads down the slope at top speed while smacking his right buttock with an imaginary jockey's whip and gurgling, "And with two furlongs to go it's Cherry Tunes from Victory V with Fisherman's Friend Original coming up on the stand side." (*figure 1*)

THE HALF-PIGGOT
As above but crouching. (*figure 2*)

3.Lone ranger style...

4. Surfer style...

5. Or slapstick fun, the choice is yours!

THE RODEO

Stander makes his woodie buck up and down by pulling on the "reins" while simultaneously waving his balaclava in the air and bellowing "Yee-hah! Ride him cowboy!" in what he imagines is an American accent. (*figure 3*)

THE BOOK HIM DANNO

Stander drops the reins and rides down "no hands" with his arms outstretched, steering by shifting the weight on his feet and singing the theme from *Hawaii Five-O.* (*figure 4*)

THE DAD

Stander sets off on an erratic, bobbing course, yells, "Stop panicking, woman, I used to do this all the time when I was a lad" and then catapults off the front, landing head first in a snow drift. (*figure 5*)

The Playground Winter Triathlon

1. Slugers pool their information and sweets

A sport that developed from Britain's need to train a generation of reservist vandals in case of another war with France, playground winter triathlon requires nerve, stamina and skill in equal measure.

Playground winter triathlon is sometimes referred to as sign-luge or sluge, with competitors known as slugers, and culminates in competitors descending a grassed-over slagheap on one of those striped bars local councils use to fence off holes in the road.

TRIATHLON (FIRST PHASE)

The slugers begin the event by trying to locate a suitable bar for themselves using their skill, judgement and bits of information passed on by "that fat kid whose granddad works on the bins". This phase requires navigation skills as well as the ability to extract information using offers of Bazooka bubblegum, a chance to look at the naughty playing cards your Dad has in his hankie drawer and Chinese burns.

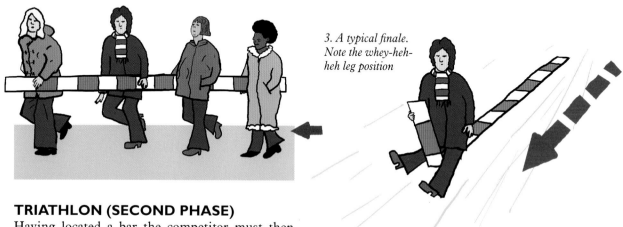

2. Stealth, speed and teamwork are essential!

3. A typical finale. Note the whey-heh-heh leg position

TRIATHLON (SECOND PHASE)

Having located a bar the competitor must then steal it and smuggle it to the downhill course evading police patrols and council workmen, and stopping every half-mile to let off a volley of abuse at anybody who asks, "And where d'you think you are off to with that, you little hooligan?" Time deductions are awarded for accuracy and the closeness of "F" word clusters (or "Tynans" as they are known to the sluge fraternity).

TRIATHLON (THIRD PHASE)

Once at the course the competitors bend the front of the bar up to form a streamlined shield, sit on it and slide down the slope repeatedly, the winner being one who wears a groove in the snow so deep that mud shows through it in the shortest possible time.

Snowballing

Balling has been a feature of the winter playground since Renaissance times. During the 19th century the game divided into two distinctly different sports: combat balling and artistic (or giant) balling.

COMBAT BALLING

Combat balling is a rugged no-nonsense sport that sees two teams hurling snowballs at one another from distances of up to five yards. The rules of the sport may vary from region to region but all events that are sanctioned by National Combat Balling Association must comply with the following by-laws:

(a) Teams must be of roughly equal size, unless one is obviously winning in which case all late arrivals will join that one.

(b) Snowballs must be made from snow not slush.

(c) Snowballs may not be dipped in water to make them icy.

(d) Snowballs may not have gravel in them.

(e) The last three laws may be ignored if the opposition is from a rival school and last year "did our Gary over even though he was on his own and there were masses of them".

(f) No deliberate throwing of snow down the tops of opponents' wellingtons.

(g) Extra "coup" points are scored by any individual who manages to "explode" a ball off the back of a grown-up's head "by accident, mister, honest. I was aiming at Kev."

(h) The contest ends when one of the team is so cold their fingers have gone blue and they start to cry. Their opponents are then declared the winner and both teams rush into the cloakroom and stick their hands on the radiator to warm them up while discussing how they once saw a programme on telly about a bloke in America who got frostbite and his toes started to smell like rotten meat and he had to cut them off with a penknife.

Caretaker

Team B

Grass trails

Team A

ARTISTIC (GIANT) BALLING

A sport that has the benefit of providing entertainment for children of all ages and both sexes. Teams of artistic ballers are gathered together when one "skipper" begins rolling a snowball along and chanting "All join on, all join on". As others group around him or her they increase the rolling speed and strength of the group. Once two or three groups have begun rolling a contest to build the "most massive snowball ever" begins in earnest.

Above – A size-ball contest in full swing. The competing teams have each rolled up large snowballs though it looks like team B will be disqualified for bulking out their ball using one of the titchy kids from Mrs McConnell's class. The arrival of Mr Sullen the caretaker shouting, "Get off the bloody field, you little swines, you're ruining the flippin' grass" signals the end of the competition. The balls will now be measured by arm-widths and a winner duly declared.

EST. 1891
STILL A FAMILY BUSINESS

MILLWARD'S

CHOCMALLOW MUNCHIES

Britain's favourite gooey marshmallow-and-chocolate-style teatime treat (with strawberry jam-type filling) are proud to provide financial aid through the Playground Sports Association to adults and children who are keen to learn how to sledge, slide and snowball more proficiently

For further details those who have qualified for free school dinners and are not too ashamed of their poverty to proclaim it publicly should write to:

MILLWARD'S PAUPER HELP ASSISTANT, SUGARBURST HOUSE, FRANGLEY, EAST RIDING OF YORKSHIRE
(Please remember to mark your envelope "Scrounger")

Circa 1898

Playground Compendium

Featuring Diving, Conkers, Best Man Dead, Girly Games (though there's not too much on them really, so don't be put off!) and quite a few more.

TSP tackle this sport

Produced In Association With Take That Tojo!
The Official Publication Of The Uk Japs And Commandos Federation

U.K. PRICE **37p net**

Playground Girly Games

THE ORIGINS

by Professor Dennis Hairpeace, social anthropologist, author of Ladywatching *and* The Frocked Monkey

When you have spent as much time as I have watching women, frequently without their knowledge, often from the branches of a tree, late at night, through special binoculars, you gain a precious and priceless insight into the female mind, as well as into the workings of the British judicial system, which frankly allows scant flexibility when it comes to judging between the serious research of committed professionals and what the constabulary choose to characterise as "the pervy doings of a dirty old bleeder".

Be that as it may, thanks to my studies I am, by common consent, the impish intellectual to turn to when a television producer or Sunday newspaper editor wants answers to those age-old questions about girly games, "What are they doing?" "How do they know who's won?" and "Why are they wearing something that looks like a skirt but is, on closer inspection, actually a pair of shorts?"

Before I set about addressing those posers let me enlighten you about something of which ordinary decent dull folk such as yourselves are generally unaware (it's nothing to be ashamed of: ignorance is perfectly natural, as natural as how's-your-father between two attractive people who are terribly fond of one another, and I can't emphasise that enough). You see, people, human beings, or *homo sapiens* if you will, don't just communicate verbally by speaking to each other, they also converse physically through the universal language I call "bodytalk".

What is bodytalk? Well, bodytalk is a mood. It's a feeling. It's something that can shoot you down in flames, or get you dancing on the ceiling. But most of all it is a common language, a non-verbal lingua franca, a corporeal pidgin as it were, that mankind developed when we were still primitive cave dwellers, or possibly even hairless apes living in communes in the leafy canopy of the mighty

Figure 1

Figure 2

jungle trees. As a result bodytalk is so embedded in our subconscious that quite often we are telling people things, sending them signals, without even realising we are doing it. For somebody fluent in bodytalk, such as myself, this can lead to some rather embarrassing situations, especially on public transport. But since that case is sub judice I shall pass no further comment on it here.

Take a look at *figure 1:* an ordinary school playground scene.

Now look at *figure 2:* a typical group of chimpanzees. Strip away the background details and the resemblance is uncanny, isn't it?

Notice anything else in that first picture of the kids? Yes, the boys are wearing trousers, while the girls wear skirts. The reason for these garment choices is subliminal and actually stretches way back into primordial times when the male homo sapien was a shaggy hunter-gatherer eager to bring back a big slice of woolly mammoth as an offering to the fur-bikini-clad object of his affections. The boys you see are the hunters, and they have covered their legs in a bid to convince their prey that they don't actually have any. Look – the trousers proclaim cunningly – we have torsos and feet, but our lower limbs have disappeared. This was one of the many ruses that allowed primitive man to flourish. Because, believe me, no animal is afraid of a legless predator, and so the hunters – legs camouflaged – were able to approach within spear range and make their kill.

The girls are not hunters, naturally. In fact, they are often the hunted. And so they are showing the hunters (i.e. the boys) their hind limbs. This is as a means of signalling: "We have legs, so we can run away from you." Modern miniskirts as worn by supple young actresses such as Judy Geeson or Elke Sommer reveal more leg, thus emphasising the length of those ladies' limbs. They are saying, in effect: "Look how long my legs are. There's no chance a little shorty fella like you can catch me. In order to do that you will need an E-type Jag like what that Georgie Best has got." And thanks to regular appearances in publications like this I do. And it's red too. Grrrrrrr!

Now let's turn our attention to playground games. Here's a diagram of the average school playground at break-time.

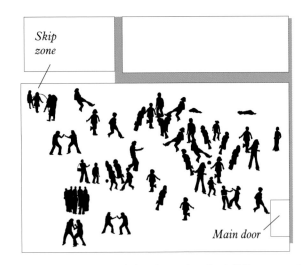

Skip zone

Main door

The playground is the school child's natural habitat. Notice if you will how the boys' games spread all over the majority of that "territory", while the girls confine themselves to a tiny corner. Sometimes the girls may try and edge out a little towards the middle of the yard, but they will soon be driven back by cries of "Oi, you're stood in our penalty area. Go on, sling your hook, or you'll likely get a ball in the cakehole and run off blubbing to Mrs Gribble."

Why has this situation arisen? Members of the so-called "Women's Liberation" movement (or Women's Glib as I mischievously call it) will no doubt say it is because men are selfish and bossy and regard the female of the species as intrinsically inferior. Nothing could be further from the truth. In fact, the boys and girls are simply acting upon the instructions of their subconsciouses. As I explained before, man is "the hunter" and in order to hunt he must roam far and wide – as the boys are doing in this diagram. The female by contrast is a "nester" and therefore stays in a small familiar area, often one she has made especially cosy using air fresheners and brightly coloured cushions made from the feathers of exotic parrots.

We can see further evidence of the difference between boys and girls in the summer games they play. Boys play cricket, a game in which they register points by running up and down in straight lines, while the girls play rounders in which they register points by running round in a circle. It is clear from this that, though they are totally unaware of it, the two sets of players are complying with some primitive urge, pre-programmed deep within the psyche – the boys tracing the rigid line of a man's thingummy, while the girls trace the curved outline of the mummy's tummy.

We have football clubs and knitting circles. Need I say more?

Other cultures do things differently, of course. In the USA, for example, men play baseball in which they register scores by sprinting round a diamond-shaped field. This shows the malign and repressive influence of religion in that country. The men are simply too embarrassed and ashamed to play cricket. I firmly believe that should the day arrive when Americans are able to discuss hanky-panky and monkey-business in the sort of honest, adult way we do here in modern Britain, then they will surrender to their primitive urges and give up baseball for good.

Dennis Hairpiece

French Skipping

As its name implies, French skipping* was invented by French people from the naval port of Toulon. The sport began as a form of deck exercise for sailors who would "perform many fancy steps upon the stretched garters of their sweethearts" while their ship was at sea.

French skipping remained popular in France and was spread throughout Europe during the era of Napoleon. It did not come to England until later in the nineteenth century, however. It was brought to these shores by French exile, poet Paul Verlaine. Attempting to forget his unhappiness about his chum Arthur Rimbaud, Verlaine engaged in long sessions of French skipping on Bournemouth seafront, where his ability to dance around bits of elastic in a mournful, introspective and strangely haunting manner impressed thousands of teenagers, many of whom thought that copying him would make them seem deep and clever. To this day British French skipping, or laggies as it is often known, still shows the symbolist influence of the author of *Sagesse*.

Napoleonic French Sailors

English ship

Above: French matelots exercise on the man o' war *Ooh La La* on the morning of the Battle of Trafalgar. Note the officer keeping watch for any violation of the laws. The notoriously finicky attitude of these gentlemen to rules infringements was the origin of the term "petty officer".

*In South Wales French skipping is called Chinese skipping. Nobody knows why. The Welsh are just awkward like that.

Chanters / Endos / Our Michelle / Skipper / TBTGWBI

French skipping is a game of technical skill and gymnastic grace in which the girls execute a series of complex exercises inside, outside and on the elastic at a variety of designated heights commencing with anklesies and moving up to kneesies, thighsies and so on. The exact rules of it remain obscure, but at the end of a competition a winner emerges thanks to the auspices of the judge, The Big Tough Girl Whose Brother Is In Borstal. The decision on who gets first place is based on a complex formula in which height of elastic is multiplied by number of manoeuvres successfully completed and then divided by the who-does-she-think-she-is-just-because-her-Dad-has-a-Morris-Oxford-and-driving-gloves factor.

THE POSITIONS

1. ENDO – Every game of French skips must include endos. The endos' job is to stand with the knicker elastic around the back of their legs while the skipper performs her manoeuvres, and to move

the elastic up as the difficulty levels increase. Being an endo requires good leg strength and the ability to withstand a certain amount of chafing behind the knees without making a big song-and-dance about it. Remember when choosing endos that the height of the elastic will rise as the competition goes on, so a balanced pairing is essential.

2. SKIPPER – The girl who is currently engaged "on laggy". Agility, speed, skill and the ability to jump around in a skirt without flashing your pants are key assets.

3. *CHANTERS* – While waiting for their turn to skip the other competitors clap rhythmically and chant, often singing an amusing song about boys the skipper may or may not fancy taking her "down the garden".

4. *THE BIG TOUGH GIRL WHOSE BROTHER IS IN BORSTAL* – Like her twin, The Big Tough Boy Whose Brother Is In Borstal, the Big Tough Girl Whose Brother Is In Borstal is the final arbiter on all technicalities and rules including the infamous "England, Ireland, Scotland, Wales, Inside, Outside, On" protocols. She also decides when the laggy will be "raised" to the next level. The Big Tough Girl Whose Brother Is In Borstal never skips herself. This is not because she is too fat. It is because she thinks it is daft. Oh yeah? Yeah.

5. *OUR MICHELLE* – The best friend and cousin of The Big Tough Girl Whose Brother Is In Borstal. Her role is to supply The Big Tough Girl Whose

The danger of endo imbalance. The contest has reached waistsies, if it is raised to chestsies the elastic will fire off the short endo's head, striking the tall endo a stinging blow in a sensitive area

Brother Is In Borstal with wine gums and cherry lips while helping her make her final judgement on the victor by saying things like "Our Mam saw that posho Andrea in British Homes Stores and she was buying a bra and I said, 'You what?' and my Mam said 'a bra' and I said 'A bra? What's she going to put in it, coconuts?' Cacacacacacacac-ha. Coconuts. Cacacacacacaca-ha. Eeee, I nearly wet meself."

THE EQUIPMENT

Like all of the world's greatest games French skipping requires only a minimum investment in kit, though as with everything paying for the highest-quality items your parents can afford will always pay dividends in the long run even if you do only use them twice and they end up going to the white elephant stall at the school bring-and-buy with those bloody American roller-skates you went on and on about.

The main thing you need, of course, is a twelve-foot length of knicker elastic with the ends sewn together to form a loop. Try always to buy British knicker elastic. This is not only a great help to the balance of payments deficit facing Mr Wilson and HM Government, it also makes sound sense. British is best! After all, you hardly need to have made a detailed study of the films of Brigitte Bardot or that Swedish bloke to know that Continental knicker elastic tends to be a little on the droopy side. And knicker elastics imported from behind

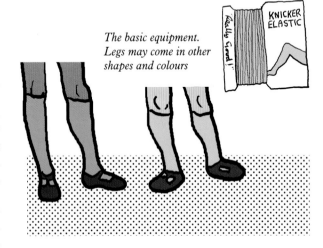

The basic equipment. Legs may come in other shapes and colours

the Iron Curtain are often Red Army military grade that is simply too powerful for safe skipping.

Above: Amazing though it seems this is all the kit you need to get involved in what the British French Skipping Society believes will be an Olympic event by 1996, even if mankind has emigrated to the moon by then as seems likely.

Always read the "breaking strain" poundage before using new knicker elastic or accidents like this one may occur

Above: An example of the perils of using Soviet knicker elastic. In the middle of an on-laggie cross-and-turn this too-firm elastic has catapulted the two endos together, catching the skipper in the middle. Note the group of boys who have rushed over from their football game because they thought it was a fight and are now milling round in the hope of seeing somebody's bum cheek.

OTHER PLAYGROUND GIRLY GAMES

Apart from French skipping there are a number of other playground girly games all of which involve clapping, chanting and generally being nice and smelling of apple blossom. However, the distaff side have already taken up more space than is strictly necessary, so we're not going to say anything about those.

Playground Diving

By Brian "Mighty Dosher" Gawthorpe, Yorkshire
Springboard Champion

If you've watched the Olympic Games ever you'll have got the impression that diving is a load of little, skinny blokes trying to jump into a swimming baths making the least noise and splash possible, so as not to frighten the tiny tots. Watching such rubbish fair makes me sick. I mean, it makes diving look like something only the sort of weeds who hang around with the dinner-lady all playtime talking about *Crossroads* would go in for. Which is not the case. Not round here, any road. After all, anybody who's not gone completely doolally knows that the whole point of diving is to do a blooming great Tarzan yell and then smack down into the pool with a sound like somebody whacking a cow's backside with a wet blanket. And the more water that goes over the edge of the baths the better the dive. Simple as that.

COMPETITION PLAYGROUND DIVING

Most folk just do their playground diving for a bit of a laugh and to splash that so-called "lifeguard" Trevor Dish because he really fancies himself, strutting up and down, puffing out his chest, smiling at the lasses and blowing that bloody whistle every two seconds. Some though take playground diving a little more seriously and enter competitions both here in the UK and abroad.

The typical domestic diving competition is a simple thing that generally begins down the baths of a Saturday morning when a new lad has appeared from out of town, possibly down south or somewhere because he's got funny hair, and a few of us start saying, "I bet you daren't jump off the top board. I bet you daren't. I bet you daren't. You cowardy custard."

He responds by saying, "I do dare, I do. I'm a right nutter, me. You don't believe me, do you? I am a nutter, I am, me."

After these preliminaries the contest proper can

Incorrect diving

Correct diving

begin, no holds barred, Geronimo-option in operation, first one to be forcibly ejected from the pool by the attendants the winner. Straight ahead brilliant.

Continental competitions are somewhat different from this, basically because you are the new lad from out of town and they are the ones that start shouting at you, usually in foreign, so you can't tell if they're being nice or not, but it's generally wisest to think the worst in my opinion because that way you don't walk off giving them the feeling they've made a right Charlie out of you.

To be honest, though, the continent is no place for a novice diver, as anybody who has seen the European champ, Volker "The Hammelbach Torpedo" Straub, completely empty an Olympic-size pool with a single bellyflop will testify. If you ever want to see what diving is really all about, try and catch that lad in action one afternoon on *World of Sport*. They say he displaces more water than a Yank aircraft carrier and his bloodcurdling springboard yell fair rips the roof off the changing rooms. The bloke's a human depth charge. I can't pay him a bigger compliment than saying that I only wish Straubie was British. And I bet he does too.

Playground Combat Games

(a)

By Brigadier Jock Sausage (ret)

Sadly, there are an increasing number of people – many of them women, admittedly – who reject the idea of war as a good clean bit of masculine fun. Constantly harping on about casualties, amputees and human suffering, they make out that armed combat is nothing but an appalling waste of human life. Now don't get me wrong, war is hell. But if the alternative is sitting at home trying to do the *Daily Telegraph* crossword while lifting both feet in the air so the old girl can get the vacuum cleaner under the settee and deal with the biscuit crumbs, well, I ask you, what fellow with an ounce of spunk is going to plump for option B?

Thank goodness then for the playground, a place where there are still plenty of plucky young fellows who believe that fighting the Nazis was a rip-roaring game filled with splendid explosions, bloodcurdling battle cries and wizard bayonet charges, and at the end of the day everybody shook hands and went home for a splendid tea of sardines on toast and junket. As somebody who served from Dunkirk to Suez all I can say is it sets my mind at ease to think that the proud tradition of Britain's military disasters is being passed over into hands such as these.

BEST MAN DEAD

A splendidly simple game this and one that places the proper emphasis on the absolute importance of dying in as spectacular a manner as possible to entertain your comrades.

The players line up and, when called by the final arbiter of all things (The Big Tough Boy Whose Brother Is In Borstal), each shouts out the weapon by which he is about to be killed and then enacts the appropriate death scene. Popular choices are:

(a) *SUB-MACHINE GUN* – Dying man is hit by bursts of automatic fire causing him to leap and twitch across the playground before gripping the litter-bin post and sliding down it gradually with his tongue hanging out. Extra marks awarded for quality of sub-machine gun noise. Let's really see some genuine differences between the trusty old Thompson SMG and Jerry's infernal Schmeisser.

(b) *HAND GRENADE* – Dying man watches in horror as hand grenade comes towards him, rushes towards it in the hope of throwing it back towards the enemy, but alas... The explosion causes him to jump high in the air and land in a crumpled heap. His last act is to point towards the enemy and croak, "You'll never beat us, Fritz."

(c) *AMBUSHED IN THE JUNGLE BY MILLIONS OF JAPANESE SOLDIERS* – Dying man cuts his way through thick foliage without realising that a sly and cunning enemy surrounds him. Shots ring out on all sides causing him to stumble in many directions, knocking over the dustbins by the science lab and bouncing off Mrs Grimble the dinner lady, before coming to rest in the entrance to the boys' toilets. As the light dims he calls out, "Leave me here, lads. I'll only hold you up," causing several witnesses to sob manfully into their hankies.

After all contestants have enacted their death scene the Big Tough Boy Whose Brother Is In Borstal chooses the winner. His decision is based on artistic merit, dramatic effect and who did his maths homework for him last.

Outnumbered six-to-one, the ideal odds

JAPS AND COMMANDOS

This game has always been a puzzle to those of us who have made a study of World War Two because, of course, the commandos were never deployed in the Far East. Nevertheless the idea of pitting this elite British fighting unit against the Japanese does have a certain appeal and one sincerely hopes that at some point in the future the politicians will get their fingers out and give us the chance to see it for real.

THE GAME – Now clearly in a game of Japs and Commandos there can be only one winner – the British (and don't any of you Lefties start up about Singapore or I shan't be held responsible for my actions, believe me). Nevertheless those selected to be the Japs (that is to say little brothers, weeds, milksops and any of that type of girl who like to wear trousers and neglect their nails) can still put up a good show and earn themselves an honourable defeat. A game of Japs and Commandos takes place during breaktime and any number of people can take part, though clearly it is better if the commados are hopelessly outnumbered as that will add lustre to their victory.

The game begins when the Japs launch their attack, charging across the playground uttering piercing war cries and yelling, "You die, white dogs". The commandos respond by unleashing a devastating barrage of fire including the unmistakable "naaaaa-nanananananananana-nah" sound of the Sten gun. Some Japs fall instantly to the ground, rolling about and groaning, but others rush on undeterred by the sound of explosions and the fact the ice-cream van has just arrived at the school gates. The commandos respond to this second wave with another deadly burst of fire and yells of "I hit you. You're dead. Stop running. I just killed you!" To which the Japs respond with some fire of their own and shouts of "No you didn't. You missed. You can't shoot straight. Ha-ha-ha." At this point a genuine fight breaks out and Puffy Padmore has to come running from the staff room bawling, "Stop that at once. What is this blasted noise? It sounds like World War Three out here." Which shows how little he knows.

EQUIPMENT

Johnny Seven machine gun   *Luger*   *Revolver*

Ray-gun   *Spud-gun*   *Piece of wood*

Tennis ball

Colander   *Tin can*   *Cindy doll*   *Grannie's walking stick*

A range of weapons that can be deployed in a game. The can, tennis ball and piece of wood are used as hand grenades, while the rest are firearms. The colander can be worn as a helmet

Conkers

Conkers is a game played by two people armed with a horse chestnut attached to a length of string.

COLLECTING YOUR CHEGGIES

The first move for anybody who wants to get involved in the sport is to find some conkers. These can generally be located at the bottom of a horse chestnut tree in October. Please only gather nuts that have fallen from the tree naturally. Never throw things into the branches in an attempt to dislodge them. This can harm the tree and may also lead to the man across the road coming running out of his house yelling, "That bloody stick you just hoyed nearly hit my new Morris Oxford, you ruddy little twerp" and threatening to remove his belt and smack your bottom with it.

TYPES OF CHEGGY

THE THROUGHBRED – The racing stallion of the horse chestnut world. Large and shiny, it positively glows with vigour. Sadly in combat it will shatter at the first blow.

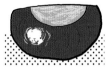

THE DISH – The strange, flattened Frankenstein's monster's head appearance of this cheggy along with its sharp-looking edges may give the newcomer the impression that it will be a handy fighter. Nothing could be further from the truth. It will be smashed to smithereens as easily as blinking.

 *THE BATTLING BANTAM* – Hardly bigger than a pea, the BB doesn't look like much but his tiny size makes him extremely difficult to hit and he will gradually wear a bigger opponent down with his flurries of light tapping blows.

 THE OLD FAITHFUL – Don't be fooled by his appearance, this old boy is the ultimate conkering machine and the choice of all top champions. Sir Robert Peel's legendary Victorian 249-er, Wrinkly Wilfred, is now in the Natural History Museum, London. Left for 12 months in Nan's airing cupboard the Old Faithful is as tough as teak and virtually unbreakable. Will only lose in a contest with another of his ilk. Such fights are long and violent wars of attrition that often go on till way past your bedtime.

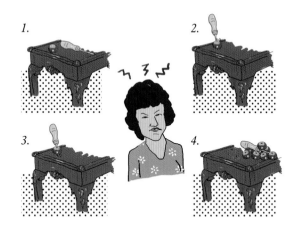

PIERCING YOUR CONKER

Once you have your conkers the next thing to do is to make a hole through them from top to bottom. This is best done with a bradawl, electrician's screwdriver or one of your Mum's knitting needles. Try to do the piercing on a solid surface such as the mahogany dining table or the top of one of the new Hygena QA kitchen units. This way the gouges that result will stay as a permanent reminder of the conker season long after the huge amount of shouting and bawling that followed their discovery has died away.

STRINGING YOUR CONKER

Now you have a conker with a hole in it the next thing to do is to string it. There are a number of types of string you can use but experience has shown that by far the best is the shoelace. Prince of all shoelaces is the leather shoelace. You will usually find these in your Dad's best brogues, the ones he only ever gets out of the wardrobe for weddings, funerals and job interviews. Because he doesn't use them very often he is unlikely to notice the laces are missing for several months (and only then when he is in a right tearing hurry because the bloomin' alarm clock failed to go off and he has spent 20 minutes looking for his cufflinks), but it is wise to check the calendar on the mantelpiece just to be on the safe side.

If you can't find a leather shoelace then use an ordinary lace taken from any of those shoes you don't like wearing because they rub the back of your heels and make you look posh. Alternatively you can use a length of orange baler twine (you can find this in most hedges). Carefully force one end of your string through the hole using your screwdriver, knitting needle or bradawls, being extra careful to make a few more scratches on the table or work surface.

Once the string is safely through tie a knot in it. Remember to make the knot as big as possible. This will help protect your conker against sneaky underarm attacks and also prevent it coming off when you make a violent swipe, flying across the playground and striking Mrs Gout the cook on the back of the head while she is clearing plates into the slop bucket to take round to her brother Alf and his pigs.

THE CONTEST

The North West Horse Chestnut Sports Association operates its tournaments under the hit-until-you-miss rule. Some other regions favour the three-strikes law, but we feel that does not reward skill and accuracy. In fact, of course, as all cheggiers of any experience know when it comes to conkers, hitting is much the same as being hit.

"STAMPS"

Another rule which helps liven up what is, admittedly, already a game too thrilling to be televised (or that's what the head of ITV sport told us when we approached him about a regular slot on *World of Sport*, or alongside bar billiards and table football on *Indoor League* with FS Trueman) is that of "stamps". "Stamps" allows the opponent of anyone whose conker hits the ground to chase after it calling "stamps!" and attempting to crush it underfoot, while the owner scrabbles about trying to retrieve it and avoid getting his fingers broken.

Check before stamping! Legitimate in some areas, in others this action may be regarded as foul play

The non-aficionado may think it unlikely that anyone would drop his conker during competition, but a gifted player can use "strings" (a shot in which the respective conker laces become entwined) to disarm his adversary with a sudden twirl of the wrist in the manner of D'Artagnan. Or at least he can unless his opponent has wound the lace round his fist. In this case any attempt to spin or tug the conker from his grasp simply draws the lace around the knuckles until they are as tight as a tourniquet. On a frosty autumn morning this produces the kind of sharp, icy pain traditionally associated with unrequited love.

The winning conker, of course, inherits all the previous victories of the defeated nut. If a two-er beats a six-er it becomes an eight-er and so on. We can't help thinking this scoring system might profitably be adopted by other sports. Imagine the thrills and drama that would be brought to the Football League, for instance, if the winners not only picked up two points for a victory but also all their beaten opponent's points too. Neither Leeds United, nor rivals Derby County, Liverpool and Manchester City would feel so confident, if they knew that defeatin the last game of the season at Selhurst Park would condemn them to relegation and propel Crystal Palace to the title.

CONKERS UNDER THREAT

Unbelievable though it may seem there are some do-gooder, social worker types who believe conkers is dangerous. They cite occasions on which the odd child has been struck on the head by flying cheggies or the falling branches of trees from which he has been attempting to extract some likely looking nuts. We feel we must speak out against this attempt to undermine our ancient sport. After all, what kind of society is it that values sharp cognitive faculties more highly than interesting head wounds? Not one in which we at NWHCSA would want to live, that's for certain.

FURTHER INFORMATION

If you want to know more about conkers then you should write to your local club or association (remember to include a stamped addressed envelope). The details and addresses of organised conkers in your area will generally be found in your local library or on a postcard stuck with sticky tape onto the window of the newsagents next to the adverts for carpet cleaners and second-hand fondue sets. Always ask your mother or father before using the telephone. You will need somebody big and strong to help you turn the dial.

If you've enjoyed this book you may be interested

THE YOUNG EXECUTIVE COLLECTION

The latest range of know-how volumes from the brains behind Tackle This Sport. Aimed at newlyweds who have just moved into one of the attractive modern housing estates that are springing up on the outskirts of Britain's towns and cities, The Young Executive Collection spells out in words and diagrams how to organise your home and social life in a stylish modern manner.

Published so far:
Entertaining With Fondue
Have Fun With Fablon
The Mateus Rose Story
Getting The Best From Onyx

Coming soon:
Arranging Your Coffee Table
Decorating With Shells
The Avocado –
    And What To Do With It
Wife Swapping For Fun and Fitness